Standardizing Storage Management

Using the Veritas Storage Foundation to increase the effectiveness of storage management across the enterprise

Sean Derrington

Josh Kahn

Paul Massiglia

Symantec Corporation 20330 Stevens Creek Blvd. Cupertino, CA 95014 USA

http://www.symantec.com

ISBN 0-321-447794

Acknowledgments

Our goal in writing this book has been to articulate the value proposition for storage management standardization, and to show how the Veritas Storage Foundation by Symantec can make standardized management of online storage a reality in large and heterogeneous data centers. We were aided in this task by Sean Derrington, of Symantec's Data Center Management Group, who formulated the basic ideas of standardization for us.

We are particularly grateful to Manish Parekh and Aglaia Kong of the Storage Foundation Management Server group for access to test systems for use in developing Chapter 6, as well as to Distinguished Engineers Craig Harmer and Ron Karr for their painstaking technical reviews of the VxFS file system and VxVM volume manager material respectively. Also to DCMG Technology Strategy VP John Colgrove, who continually reminded us that "this is the most important book of the series."

As any author knows, creating the content of a book is only part of the challenge. We thank Sarah Connell-Smith of the Symantec Infodev organization for her third great Yellow Book editing job in as many months. LMA Associates provided quick and accurate turnaround of the graphics. Symantec's production team, in particular, Jim Hudgens, Fran Heddings, and Rossana Monzon did quick and accurate conversions from raw manuscript to camera-ready images, whipped out cover art in next to no time, all while they were trying to be accommodating to undisciplined and tardy authors.

Finally, our special thanks to our project manager Kristine Mitchell, whose persistence and good humor as we all learned together how Symantec takes a book from raw manuscript to finished product are responsible in large measure for *Standardizing Storage Management* finding its way into your hands.

If despite the extraordinary efforts of this team, errors and omissions remain, responsibility for them lies solely with the authors.

Sean Derrington
Josh Kahn
Paul Massiglia

Mountain View, CA
April, 2006

Contents

Chapter 1

The what and why of standardized storage management

This chapter includes the following topics:

- Why manage storage?
- What is storage management?
- The Veritas Storage Foundation by Symantec

Why manage storage?

"Storage is free!"

This obviously overblown argument is heard frequently in many contexts, from personal computer users to enterprise storage system salespeople to application designers bent on storing every bit of data that might, just possibly, be valuable some day. The usual justification is to point to the dramatic and continuing decrease in magnetic disk prices, and in the case of the data center, new storage network interconnect technologies that promote large scale flexible deployment, and the availability of multiple "tiers" of cost-differentiated storage.

But as CIOs, IT directors, and system administrators know all too well, storage isn't free—not even close. Particularly for large enterprises, storage is a significant contributor to overall information technology cost for three main reasons:

- Today, the hardware and software required to package, power, cool, and manage large numbers of disk drives usually exceeds the cost of the drives themselves. Add to this the cost of floor space and HVAC, and disk drives become an even smaller contributor to the overall lifetime cost of online storage.

- Storage consumption is growing, and the growth shows no signs of abating. So much business value can be derived from storing and analyzing data about so many topics that storage consumption is increasing faster than unit cost is decreasing.
- Storage management is personnel-intensive, and personnel is the one information technology cost that increases rather than decreasing over time. Storage must be managed, and larger amounts of storage require more management. Hardware must be inventoried, repaired when it breaks, and periodically replaced with newer models. Raw disk capacity must be configured and provisioned to application servers (which are also growing in number). The "right" data must be placed on the "right" type of storage devices. Data must be protected against a variety of threats to loss or destruction. Storage management is personnel-intensive, and personnel is the one information technology cost that can be relied upon to increase rather than decrease over time.

Online storage growth

The analyst group Forrester Research had this to say in its US information technology spending forecast for the second quarter of 2005:

"The strongest budget growth in 2005 and 2006 will be computer equipment. Total US spending in this area will rise 12% in 2005 and 13% in 2006. The growth is the result of investments in personal computers, storage hardware, and blade servers in 2003, 2004, and so far in 2005, as companies upgraded their computing equipment after the fallow period of the tech depression from 2001 to 2002." (September 23, 2005, "US IT Spending In Q2 2005: Still Tracking Forecast," by Andrew Bartels. Quoted by permission.)

Forrester's European outlook was similar:

"When looking at hardware investments, only storage and server hardware will generate increased demand for more than 30% of firms. Compared with this, demand for IT services like consulting or application management outsourcing will remain moderate."(December 20, 2005 "Europe's IT Spending Outlook For 2006," by Manuel Ángel Méndez. Quoted by permission.)

These, and similar forecasts, suggest strongly that the amount of storage in enterprise data centers will continue to grow. More storage means more capital outlay and more operating expense. As storage cost becomes a more significant part of IT capital and operational spending, enterprises look for ways to minimize it. Two primary techniques for minimizing the overall cost of online storage have emerged:

- Using storage networks to increase deployment flexibility and therefore improve utilization. The ability to shift excess storage capacity from where it is to where it is needed with the click of a mouse rather than physical reconfiguration allows enterprises to plan for requirements that are unpredictable at best.

- Using cost-differentiated tiers of storage hardware to reduce average storage cost. Both the technology in a storage system and the configurations in which capacity is delivered to users can affect the cost of effective capacity. Mirrored storage, for example, costs at least twice as much per gigabyte as non-redundant storage. Similarly, capacity delivered via the low-cost disk drives that are appearing in so-called "nearline" storage systems can cost a fraction of the same capacity delivered using high-performance drives.

Both of these techniques are undeniably effective, but both imply that storage must be managed. To shift storage capacity from servers where it is in excess to others where it is needed, administrators must have an accurate, up-to-the-minute picture of how all storage in the data center is deployed. With individual disk arrays capable of presenting upwards of a thousand logical units (LUNs), and with data centers moving from a few enterprise-class systems to large numbers of single-application servers, tracking how storage is configured and how it is being used by applications is a full-time job, requiring multiple administrators in larger data centers.

Similarly, deploying multiple tiers of storage is effective at reducing overall cost. For example, if 80% of a data center's online data can justifiably be kept on storage configured as RAID5 rather than mirrored, overall storage cost can be reduced by 30% with no hardware configuration change. If low-cost "second-tier" disk drives can be phased in to store less-critical data, average storage cost can be reduced still further. But in achieving these cost savings, administrators must ensure that critical data is placed on redundant storage devices and frequently-accessed data is placed on high-performing devices. With millions of files in hundreds of file systems serving dozens of applications, and with the value of individual files constantly changing, using storage tiers effectively becomes a non-trivial management challenge. These, and other tasks related to the management of large amounts of storage and large numbers of files, represent the second major storage cost factor—the cost of administering storage and the data on it.

The human cost of managing storage and data

When data center storage is acquired and installed, the cost cycle is just beginning. Storage doesn't just sit there; it, and the data on it, must both be actively managed. The increasing frequency of re-provisioning (configuration of raw storage and network resources and assignment to particular hosts) has already been mentioned. In addition, storage devices and disk arrays have finite lifetimes, so regular hardware replacement and the consequent migration of data to newer hardware is necessary.

The data on storage devices must also be managed. It must be backed up regularly to protect against complete loss; periodic disk-based snapshots of critical elements must be taken to provide fast recovery from corruption if it is ever required; files must be relocated when their business value changes so that the cost of keeping a file online remains commensurate with its business value, and so forth.

As data centers grow and become more complex internally, the level of skill required to manage storage and data increases as well. In fact, data center storage architecture and management have both emerged as separately identifiable information technology career specialties. The industry analysis web site SearchStorage.com had this to say in its 2005 annual salary survey:

"Although IT management jobs continue to reign as the highest-paying positions across the technology career spectrum, storage-related positions are beginning to make inroads as well, reflecting the continued importance of data management across corporate America. Data has continued its explosive growth at many enterprises, and companies have responded by hiring in sectors that are dedicated to managing and organizing corporate data, particularly in the storage arena.

According to the TechTarget annual Salary Survey, which draws on salary numbers from across the TechTarget family of Web sites, two new entrants into the top 10 list of titles are storage-related. Storage architect, which has leapt from nowhere to score the number three spot, behind only CIOs and Internet architects, reports an average salary of $83,368, and average total compensation of $88,763. The position of storage manager has also appeared on the list for the first time. Coming in at number 8, the job has an average salary of $74,400, with average total compensation coming in at $76,300.

The rising importance of storage-related jobs makes sense, as companies continue to realize the importance of maintaining a solid and reliable infrastructure, and are investing accordingly."

(http://searchstorage.techtarget.com/originalContent/0,289142,sid5_gci1002817,00.html)

This report suggests both that staff positions specifically responsible for the storage and management of data are appearing in IT organizations, and that enterprises value the positions highly, and compensate them correspondingly. Given this, it is reasonable to expect the personnel cost of storage management to be an increasing component of data center budgets over time. Following that premise to its logical conclusion, it makes sense to explore possibilities for minimizing the human component of storage management cost.

What is storage management?

It is fashionable to measure storage management cost in terms of the number of terabytes that can be managed by a single administrator. While there is some justification for this approach, it tends to understate the full cost of storage management by relegating certain important tasks, such as backup and recovery, snapshot management, file placement and relocation, and so forth, to the application or system management domain rather than the storage management domain. A more accurate way of assessing the human cost of storage management would be to classify the administrative tasks it entails, regardless of who performs them, and explore possibilities for simplifying them.

The administrative tasks that fall under the heading of storage management generally deal with a range of objects:

- Storage hardware devices (disk drives and disk arrays)
- Storage network components (switches, routers, and host bus adapters)
- Virtual storage, whether host-, network-, or disk array-based
- File systems and the files they contain

One can argue that databases, as repositories of digital information, are a fifth type of storage management object. Although database administration is a very well-developed IT specialty in its own right, it is, in fact, postulated upon the assumption that files, virtual storage devices, and disk drives and LUNs are actually used to hold database data.

The impact of the horizontal information technology industry

Because of the way in which the enterprise information technology vendor community has evolved in recent years, each layer of the storage stack, including hardware, network components, and software, is usually delivered by different vendors, each of whom strives to be "best-in-class" for the layer occupied by their products. Worse yet, some enterprises select and deploy storage on a per-project basis rather than for the enterprise as a whole. In this environment, enterprises effectively act as their own system integrators, at least to some degree. Additionally, each element in the storage-application chain is typically managed by tools supplied by its vendor or by some third party. If a data center is home to two or more UNIX platforms, different tools are typically required for each platform.

From a storage management standpoint, proliferation of vendors, and the proliferation of tools that implies means higher cost. For example, for each storage and storage network hardware vendor whose products are present in a data center, the enterprise needs:

- A service and sparing contract with the vendor, including an enforceable service level agreement
- Training and on-going expertise in user-level management operations, such as LUN configuration

Similarly, for each system platform in the data center, the enterprise needs:

- A service and sparing contract with the vendor, including an enforceable service level agreement
- Training and on-going expertise in general system administration
- Storage-specific training and on-going expertise in platform vendor-supplied management tools (for example, logical disk managers, native file systems, and so forth)

Finally, and perhaps most expensively, for each specialized storage management software package in use in the data center, such as volume managers, snapshot managers, replicators, storage network path managers, and so forth, the enterprise needs:

- A service contract with the vendor, including an enforceable service level agreement
- Training and on-going expertise in the use of the package on each type of hardware on which it runs or with which it interfaces

Even from this brief list it is clear that enterprise storage management requires a significant number of relationships with hardware and software vendors, all of which consume administrative time and effort. Maintaining up-to-date expertise in a broad range of technologies consumes even more administrative time and effort. Intuitively, it seems that reducing the number of vendors present in the data center, or looked at another way, standardizing the components used to deliver common IT services like storage, would tend to reduce the human cost of storage management, thereby increasing the number of terabytes that an administrator could manage effectively.

Approaches to reducing storage management complexity

There are two basic approaches to reducing the complexity caused by the number of vendors present in a data center:

- Limit the number of different vendors and products present as discussed in the preceding section.
- Employ versatile hardware and software components that can serve many purposes.

Reducing the number of vendors present in the data center seems attractive at first glance. The fewer vendors that are present, the more equipment and service each vendor supplies, and the more important the enterprise becomes to the vendor as a customer. But reducing the number of vendors has a major drawback, usually called "vendor lock-in." The more dependent on a vendor's equipment a data center becomes, the more difficult and disruptive it is to displace that vendor's products and services in favor of lower cost, more advanced technology, or more advantageous relationships with other vendors. Arguably, this attitude on the part of users is what has led to the evolution of the information technology industry into horizontal tiers of "best in class" vendors.

In the long term, a more effective approach to minimizing storage management complexity and cost is to seek out hardware and software components that provide a wide range of management capabilities for the majority of the computing and storage platforms in use in a data center. The recent trend toward server virtualization is a manifestation of this. The server virtualization concept is to create a number of equivalent system environments, often running Windows or Linux, that can be deployed interchangeably as needed in departmental or other limited-scale applications.

But not all applications run on all platforms, and the most critical applications tend to require the power and robustness of enterprise-class servers, so the presence of multiple computing platforms in enterprise data centers is inevitable for the foreseeable future.

For storage itself, standardization would seem to be simpler. The basic function of storage is to provide raw capacity for cost. And indeed, many enterprises standardize on a primary storage vendor with a secondary vendor as a hedge against lagging technology or disadvantageous pricing. But recently, storage system vendors have introduced disk arrays that utilize desktop-like disk drives to reduce the cost of keeping less-critical data online. This has created a trend among enterprises to adopt "multi-tier" storage strategies. To reduce overall storage cost, enterprises accept the burden of more suppliers or more product lines, and the administrative complexity of getting the right data onto the right type of storage device.

But the greatest source of storage management complexity lies in storage and storage network management software. Storage and network suppliers provide tools for managing the components they supply. Integration of the various toolsets into a workable whole becomes a user responsibility. For data centers that use advanced storage techniques such as remote replication or snapshots of critical data, the situation is even more complex. Storage and platform vendors offer specialized tools that provide these capabilities for their own products (and sometimes for other vendors' products as well). Users must choose where in the application-storage stack these functions will be performed (for example, host-based or disk array-based replication), and which vendor's software tools will be used to perform them.

Figure 1-1 The storage management complexity issue

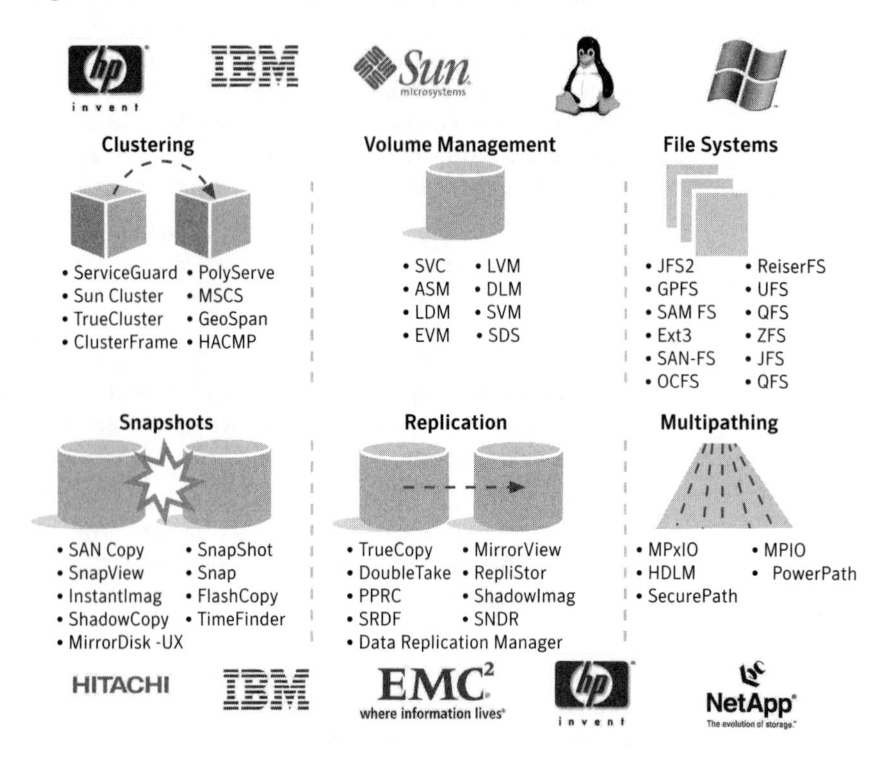

Thus, the storage management situation for most enterprise data centers, suggested graphically in Figure 1-1 may be summarized as follows:

- Multiple computing and storage system platforms are present in data centers, and will continue to be present for the foreseeable future for a variety of reasons. Important applications are platform-specific; mergers combine IT organizations with different standards and philosophies, new platform technology phases into data centers gradually, and so forth. Differentiation in cost, capabilities, and product availability makes truly homogeneous data centers impracticable.
- Most of the complexity in storage management arises not from hardware components themselves, but from the number of tools, each performing a single function for a single platform or type of storage hardware.

- Each tool incurs incremental management cost. In the short term, administrators must be trained to use it. In the longer term, the enterprise must maintain an administrative presence skilled in operating every tool for as long as it is in use.

The ideal storage management toolset

Intuitively, it seems that an effective way to attack storage management cost would be to seek out the most comprehensive set of storage management tools that provide:

- Complete functionality, both for basic functions like virtual device and file system management, as well as advanced capabilities like snapshots, remote replication, storage network path management, multi-tier storage management, and so forth
- A range of system and storage platform support, so that administrators can learn techniques once and apply the knowledge many times over
- Integration up and down the application-storage stack, so that tasks involving two or more layers, such as file system expansion or shrinkage, are accomplished in one administrative operation rather than several
- Integration with adjacent software, such as backup managers, database management systems, and low-level disk array, host bus adapter, and storage network management tools

The Veritas Storage Foundation by Symantec

The properties of the ideal storage management toolset enumerated in the preceding section are, in fact, the properties of Symantec's Veritas Storage Foundation. The Storage Foundation, described in more detail in Chapter 2, consists of a core host-based volume manager (VxVM), and file system (VxFS), as well as advanced tools for central management of storage hardware and network assets (CommandCentral) and the objects created by the Storage Foundation itself (Storage Foundation Management Server). In addition to comprehensive virtualization and file management functionality, the Storage Foundation includes advanced capabilities such as host-based remote data replication, storage network path management, and several forms of snapshots.

The Storage Foundation supports the major enterprise UNIX platforms, Solaris, HP-UX, and AIX, as well as the Red Hat and SuSE Linux server platforms. It is integrated with Symantec's NetBackup enterprise backup manager, as well as the Oracle, Oracle Real Application Cluster (RAC), DB2, and Sybase database management systems. The CommandCentral component provides interfaces to the low-level management tools supplied by all major storage and storage network hardware vendors, thereby providing complete visibility of storage and storage network resources all the way from the application to the disk drive or disk array LUN. Together, the components of the Storage Foundation comprise one of the most effective means of reducing storage management complexity and cost available to enterprises today.

The Storage Foundation value proposition

Standardizing on the Veritas Storage Foundation for all UNIX platforms in a data center attacks the problem of storage management complexity and cost head on:

- One set of tools for managing storage systems and network components for all UNIX platforms means that administrators train for and maintain their administrative skills once rather than once per computing platform or storage system type.
- One set of tools means that administrators are more versatile because they can manage storage for any platform in the data center.
- One set of tools for managing storage means greater administrator familiarity, and consequently more efficient execution with fewer errors.
- One set of tools means standardized storage management procedures, whatever hardware components are present in the data center.
- One set of tools means lower acquisition cost for storage management software.
- One set of tools means that it's easier and less disruptive to take advantage of technology and pricing trends by introducing new hardware components into the data center.
- One set of tools optimizes storage hardware investments, for example by using older disk arrays as replication targets, or by mirroring between dissimilar disk arrays.
- One set of tools means not having to maintain separate software packages and vendor relationships for every storage administration function in the data center.

In addition to reducing the cost and complexity of basic storage administration functions, the Storage Foundation opens up new possibilities for utilizing storage assets to the benefit of the enterprise:

- The Storage Foundation Dynamic Storage Tiering facility makes it possible to utilize multi-tier storage effectively without increasing administrative cost.
- Storage Foundation Space-Optimized Snapshots improve Recovery Point Objectives (RPOs) dramatically by making frequent snapshots of production data affordable.

- Storage Foundation heterogeneous mirroring and storage network management facilities simplify the migration of data between different types of disk arrays.
- Storage Foundation Portable Data Containers make it possible to process data generated on one type of UNIX platform directly on a different type of UNIX or Linux platform without network copying or cross-mounting.
- Storage Foundation Intelligent Storage Provisioning (ISP) extends an administrator's scope by automating most routine storage provisioning operations, while preserving enterprise intent for data availability and I/O performance.
- Storage Foundation Management Server centralizes the management of virtual storage, network connections, and file systems for the entire data center. From a single console, an administrator can oversee all storage objects, drilling down to individual ones to manage reconfigurations, expansions, connections, and so forth, as necessary.
- Storage Foundation Volume Server provides data center-wide visibility to host-based virtual storage, taking a big step toward data sharing by platforms of different types.
- The Storage Foundation for Databases family integrates basic Storage Foundation capabilities with major database platforms including Oracle, Oracle RAC, DB2, and Sybase, providing advanced storage services, such as snapshots and automatic file relocation, directly to the database administrator.

This book presents the case for Symantec's Veritas Storage Foundation. Chapters 3 and 4 discuss the VxVM and VxFS technologies that make up the Storage Foundation core. Chapters 5 and 6 discuss Dynamic Multi-pathing (DMP) and the Storage Foundation Management Server (SFMS) respectively. Chapter 7 presents common use cases that demonstrate the value of the Storage Foundation in everyday data center situations. Finally, Chapter 8 presents some guidelines for standardizing storage management for UNIX and Windows-based data centers.

Chapter 2

The Storage Foundation virtualization platform

This chapter includes the following topics:

- The Veritas Storage Foundation
- The VxFS file system
- Software integrated with the Storage Foundation
- What's new in the Storage Foundation

The Veritas Storage Foundation

The Veritas Storage Foundation core consists of a file system, called VxFS, integrated with a volume manager, or storage virtualizer, called VxVM. Storage Foundation software is available for major UNIX server platforms including Solaris, HP-UX, AIX, and Linux (Red Hat and SuSE). The Storage Foundation is a high-performance, scalable tool set for managing enterprise storage and data that presents a common user interface on all major UNIX platforms. Performance, scalability, and the common management interface combine with advanced functions, such as dynamic management of storage network I/O paths, to deliver the Storage Foundation's two primary value propositions:

- The lowest cost mechanism for basic management of diverse online storage and data without sacrificing function or performance
- Advanced storage management capabilities that simplify and automate storage administration and improve the quality of service delivered to data center clients

Components of the Storage Foundation

Figure 2-1 illustrates the position of the Storage Foundation in the stack of software components between business applications and data.

Figure 2-1 The Storage Foundation in the data access software stack

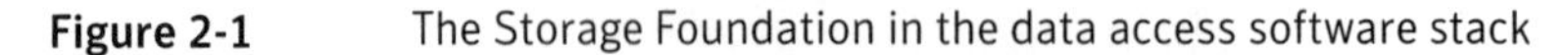

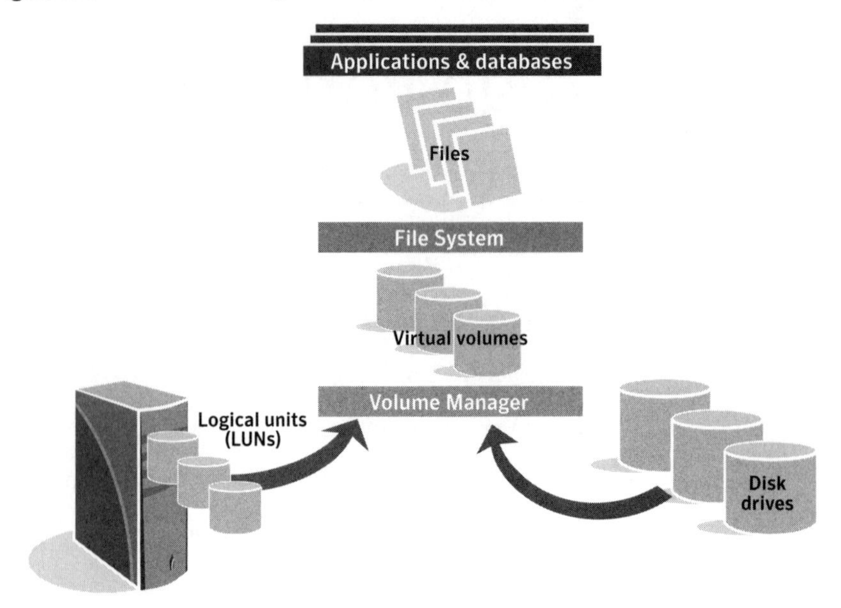

As Figure 2-1 suggests, the VxVM volume manager controls access to online storage connected to servers either directly, as is typical with disk drives, or as logical units (LUNs) presented by disk arrays over a storage network. Working through adapter and device drivers that are part of the hosting operating system, VxVM organizes the block storage of these devices and presents it upward in the form of disk drive-like virtual volumes.

Virtual volumes

The virtual volumes, usually called simply volumes, presented by VxVM appear to file systems and utilities as disk drive-like block storage devices. VxVM enhances key properties of the disk drives and LUNs it manages, improving reliability and I/O performance relative to the hardware devices that comprise them, as well as providing advanced functions not available with disk drives, such as the ability to expand or reduce the capacity of a device, or transparently transform it, for example, from RAID5 to mirrored data protection.

The disk drive-like behavior of volumes provides a powerful advantage. Nearly all storage utility programs, file systems, and database management systems are designed to manipulate data stored on disk drives. By acting like disk drives, volumes become usable by these applications and data managers with no incremental effort required to adapt them. Applications can take advantage of the superior data reliability and I/O performance delivered by virtual volumes without being specially modified to do so.

Applications and data managers like the VxFS file system that are aware of the advanced functional properties of volumes can take advantage of them. For example, on administrative command, VxFS can increase the size of the volume a file system occupies, and modify file system data structures to utilize the additional storage capacity.

Applications developed by other vendors can take advantage of VxVM volume properties as well. For example, the Oracle Disk Manager (ODM) facility can direct VxVM to read data from a particular mirror in a mirrored volume, or to bypass write logging for mirrored volumes because ODM assumes control over "resilvering" after a crash.

Volumes and LUNs

In many respects, the logical units (LUNs) of storage presented by disk arrays are similar to volumes. Both behave as disk drives from the application and data manager point of view. Both are implemented by software designed to control multiple disk drives and present upward a disk drive-like virtual device. Both enhance I/O performance and data reliability over what is available from the disks that comprise them. The LUNs presented by disk arrays differ from VxVM volumes in the six important respects listed in Table 2-1, however.

Table 2-1 Differences between LUNs and VxVM volumes

Property	Differences between VxVM volumes and disk array LUNs
Scope of applicability	The software that presents LUNs to a storage network runs in a disk array, so its scope of control is limited to disk drives within the array. VxVM runs in application or database servers, so it is able to combine any LUNs that are accessible by a server into a virtual volume, even if the LUNs are presented by different disk arrays.
Devices supported	Disk array LUNs are necessarily made up of disk drives within the array. Disk array hardware options are typically limited to two or three types of disk drive. In principle, VxVM can make use of any physical or virtual storage device presented to it by the host operating system.

Table 2-1 Differences between LUNs and VxVM volumes *(continued)*

Property	Differences between VxVM volumes and disk array LUNs
Virtual device types	Configuration options for disk array LUNs tend to be limited compared to those supported by VxVM. For example, VxVM places no practical limit on the number of mirrors (identical copies) or stripes (segments) of data on different devices, whereas most disk arrays are limited to small numbers of both.
Virtual Device Naming	Operating systems typically name disk drives and disk array LUNs according to their I/O bus or storage network addresses; administrators must usually maintain lists that correlate devices with applications and file systems. VxVM provides a flexible naming scheme with default names that relate objects to each other, as well as complete flexibility for administrators to name volumes according to application-related requirements such as their physical locations, the file systems or databases they contain, or other business purpose.
Configurations supported	Most disk arrays require that all disk drives that are part of a single LUN be of the same type. VxVM can support volumes consisting of different types of storage devices. For example, a LUN presented by an enterprise disk array can be mirrored with another presented by a different array of the same type, with a LUN presented by a different type of array, or even with a disk drive connected directly to the controlling server.
Multipath access	Disk drives in an array are typically connected to their controllers by one or two physical I/O paths. In contrast, disk array LUNs are often connected to servers by two or more storage network paths. VxVM manages multiple paths between LUNs and hosts for failure tolerance, and for disk arrays that support concurrent multipath access to LUNs, can improve performance as well.

Costs and benefits of virtual volumes

The benefits of server-based volumes do not come without a cost. Whereas the computing power to manage disk array LUNs is essentially a “sunk” cost because it is provided by the disk array’s processor, VxVM uses application server computing power to manage the volumes it presents. For most volume types, the computing power that VxVM consumes is negligible. RAID5 volumes that are subject to frequent small application writes are an exception. For these volumes, the computation and I/O required by parity updates and write logging can result in a significant small write performance differential compared to disk array-based volumes of equivalent RAID5 configuration.

The VxFS file system

The second component of the Storage Foundation core is the VxFS file system. VxFS is an advanced-function, high-performance POSIX- compliant file system for major UNIX platforms and Linux. POSIX compliance means that UNIX applications can take advantage of VxFS benefits with no modification or adaptation. Over fifteen years of development and deployment in production have made VxFS the most robust, scalable, highly-functional file system available in the UNIX and Linux environments.

Software integrated with the Storage Foundation

The value of the Storage Foundation core lies not only in features and robustness, but also in integration with other major data center software components, both from Symantec and from other vendors. Figure 2-2 represents graphically, and Table 2-2 describes the major enterprise software components with which the Storage Foundation integrates to provide comprehensive storage and file management capabilities across the data center and across the enterprise.

Figure 2-2 The Storage Foundation and related Symantec software

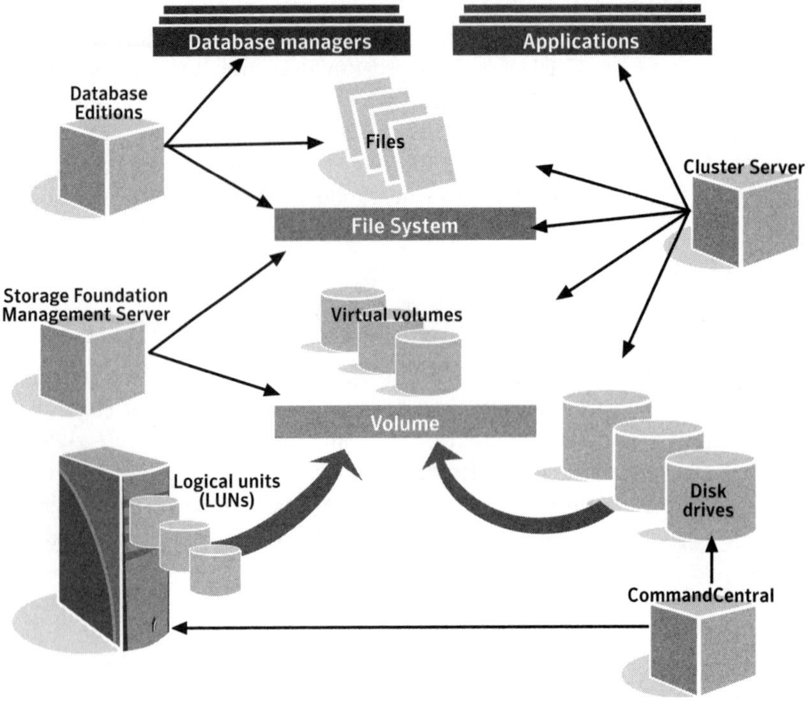

Table 2-2 Components integrated with the Storage Foundation core

Component	Description
CommandCentral	Manages and reports on Storage Area Network (SAN) components, including disk arrays and network switches and directors, from a single location (management console).
Storage Foundation Management Server	Manages and reports on Storage Foundation objects, including VxVM disk groups, volumes, and access paths, VxFS and other file systems, and groups of these objects, from a single location. In addition, consolidates the basic tasks required to provide certain higher-level services, such as migration of data between sets of disks, into higher-level services.

Table 2-2 Components integrated with the Storage Foundation core *(continued)*

Component	Description
Database Editions	Provide customized management of and reporting on Storage Foundation objects specially adapted to major database management systems, including Oracle, DB2, and Sybase. Database Editions encapsulate storage and file management tasks common to database environments so that they can be performed by database administrators (DBAs) without constant recourse to system or storage administrators.
Cluster Server	Manages applications and the resources they require to operate, including local and wide-area failover for rapid recovery from system failures and site disasters respectively.

Working in concert with these components, the Storage Foundation provides a comprehensive solution to data center and enterprise storage and file management problems; a solution whose capabilities evolve to meet the growing needs of enterprise computing as it grows in scope and becomes increasingly complex.

What's new in the Storage Foundation

The first versions of the VxVM volume manager and VxFS file system that form the core of the Storage Foundation were delivered in the early 1990s. In the fifteen-plus intervening years, the nature of UNIX-based enterprise computing has changed significantly. UNIX systems have become more powerful by several orders of magnitude, both in terms of processing ability, and in terms of multi-gigabyte primary memories that enable them to cope with more data-intensive problems. As enterprises have become comfortable with entrusting critical applications to UNIX-based systems, the number of UNIX systems in data centers has grown substantially, creating more focal points for system management, and in addition, introducing the challenge of managing changing relationships between applications and the computers they run on.

Perhaps even more significantly, online storage has moved "outside the box," and is connected to the computer systems it serves by storage networks, creating opportunities for flexible deployment and data robustness, but at the same time, introducing challenges in managing storage devices themselves, as well as the computers to which they are connected.

The Veritas Storage Foundation has kept pace with this evolution. Over the years, five major versions have been delivered, each providing increased function, scaling, and platform support compared to the one that preceded it, while preserving compatibility with users' already-installed configurations. The most recent Storage Foundation version, Version 5, improves performance and provides significant new functions, as well as responding to today's three most significant needs in enterprise storage and file management:

- A central view and point of control for all data center storage resources, provided by the Storage Foundation Management Server
- Cost-effective utilization of two or more cost-performance tiers of online data center storage, provided by the Dynamic Storage Tiering facility
- Integrated virtualization of network storage across entire data centers, provided by the Storage Foundation Volume Server

The sections that follow describe these requirements and how Storage Foundation Version 5 meets them.

Centralized storage and data management

As the number of systems and storage devices in an enterprise data center grows, simply keeping track of what installed in a data center becomes a significant challenge. With enterprise disk arrays capable of presenting thousands of LUNs to hundreds of hosts on dozens of ports, answering seemingly simple questions becomes a significant challenge:

- Which hosts are using LUNs presented by a given array?
- Which arrays are providing storage to a given host?
- Which VxVM disk groups exist in the data center and which hosts are using them?
- Which storage is VxVM protecting by mirroring, RAID5, or snapshots?
- Which file systems are mounted by which hosts and how well-utilized are they?
- Where in the data center is there underutilized storage that could be redeployed?
- What storage and file system-related alerts have been raised across the data center?
- Which storage management tasks have been performed and what were their outcomes?
- What progress is being made by long-running storage management tasks, such as data migration and volume re-layout, throughout the data center?

In a data center with one, two, or five systems, questions like this can be answered by one system administrator querying each system from its console and recording the answers. But as the number of systems and storage devices in a data center grows, storage management by spreadsheet is no longer effective. Multiple system administrators, each responsible for different applications and databases on different servers, must interact with storage administrators charged with meeting the storage needs of their applications. Storage administrators need a consistent data center-wide view of how storage is allocated and how it is being utilized, as well as a central point from which they can perform common storage management tasks such as the transfer of VxVM disk groups from one host to another, or the migration of data from one disk array to another.

Beginning with Version 5, the Storage Foundation Management Server (SFMS) capability provides administrators with global views of and comprehensive reports about all Storage Foundation objects. Moreover, SFMS makes it possible to initiate and control common storage and file system management tasks from a single console, wherever they are executed. SFMS discovers Storage Foundation objects (disks and disk groups, volumes, file systems), and related objects such as databases and managed servers, and populates a central database with their properties and states. SFMS components called agents run on systems with the Storage Foundation installed and supply information with which SFMS updates the central database as changes in the storage and data environment occur.

Storage Foundation Management Server includes reporting and monitoring components that can be used to track the state of Storage Foundation objects and respond to storage-related events, as well as active management tools that simplify the creation and execution of common storage management-related tasks.

SFMS reports can:

- Summarize overall data center storage status (for example, average utilization of storage allocated to file systems across the data center)
- Identify candidates for management action (for example, systems with the lowest utilization of the storage assigned to them, which might make them candidates for redeployment)
- Locate problem areas (for example, volumes that are stopped or at risk, or storage access paths that are interrupted or at risk of interruption if an additional component fails

SFMS alert tracking provides an overall picture of storage-related alerts so that administrators can quickly recognize, prioritize, and respond to potential problem areas before they result in application service interruptions.

Wizards supplied with SFMS guide the administrator through vitally important management tasks such as transfer of control of a VxVM disk group between hosts, or migration of data from one set of volumes to another. Wizard-based guidance minimizes both the task setup time and the potential for errors made by busy administrators under pressure to perform tasks with which they may be only marginally familiar.

In addition, recognizing that every data center's procedures are unique, SFMS makes it possible for users to store custom storage management task definitions and execute them on demand, tracking their progress through the SFMS console. Thus, for example, an administrator could define a SFMS task consisting of commands to defragment the web page file systems on all of the enterprise's web servers. The task definition could be saved in the SFMS database for execution on demand, for example whenever some external event such as a web site update was likely to have caused significant change across the web servers' file systems.

Conclusion: Storage Foundation Management Server provides a single vantage point from which administrators view all of a data center's storage virtual storage devices and file systems, and can manage them with full visibility of the consequences of actions on the entire data center storage complement.

Effective utilization of multi-tier storage

Multi-tier storage—the blending of virtual or physical storage devices with different I/O performance, data availability, and relative cost characteristics to provide differentiated online storage for computer systems—is increasingly popular among enterprise IT organizations as a way of minimizing the average cost of online storage while continuing to meet user demands.

Tiers of storage can be defined by:

- Type of hardware, for example, low-cost disk drives directly attached to hosts vs. LUNs presented by an enterprise disk array
- Age of hardware, for example, 36 gigabyte disk drives vs. 73 gigabyte disk drives in the same enterprise disk array
- Configuration, for example, RAID5 virtual devices vs. striped and mirrored virtual devices of the same capacity

All of these options deliver unique availability and performance characteristics at an associated cost. Virtualization technology allows the use of multiple technologies in combination. For example, RAID LUNs presented by two disk arrays are sometimes mirrored by VxVM or similar host-based volume managers.

Most enterprises have relatively few absolutely critical data sets. By configuring small amounts of more expensive storage for them, and relegating less critical data to less costly devices, enterprises can reduce their overall storage cost by half or more without significantly degrading the effective quality of service they deliver.

Enterprises segregate data sets for other reasons as well. For example, it is typically desirable to separate transactional data from large data streams for performance reasons, because the access patterns of the two are so different. Similarly, two data sets that are both accessed at the same time by different applications should reside on different storage devices to minimize I/O resource contention. In these and similar cases, there is benefit to be gained from segregating storage in tiers and storing different types of data on devices in a specific tier, even if all devices' capabilities are identical.

Fundamentally, enterprises organize their digital information in files. Files are closely associated with business purposes. Documents, transaction tables, images, audio and video tracks, and so forth, are all conveniently represented as files, each with a business purpose and value. This makes the file an obvious object for optimizing storage performance, availability, and cost.

To exploit multiple storage tiers, an enterprise would place each of its digital files on a type of device whose cost was commensurate with its business value. More critical files would be placed on more expensive, but higher-performing and more reliable devices; less critical files would be placed on less costly devices of presumably lower performance and reliability.

Matching one file, or a group of files, to the appropriate storage devices is not difficult. Administrators can force files to be placed appropriately, for example by assigning users or applications to file systems formatted on the appropriate types of devices. The challenge in utilizing multi-tier storage effectively lies in the numbers—placing millions of files on the right devices is far too large a task to perform effectively without some form of automation.

Moreover, the appropriate type of storage for a given file changes over time. As a file ages, is accessed more or less frequently, grows or shrinks, or moves around within its file system logical name space, the right type of storage device changes. For example, newly created transaction records are typically accessed frequently as orders are placed, scheduled for shipment, billed, and inquired about. As the records age, access is less frequent, but they must nevertheless remain online for occasional inquiries, monthly closings, data mining, and so forth. The average cost of keeping transaction records online can be reduced substantially by moving older records to lower performing, less expensive storage devices as they age and are accessed less frequently.

But manually relocating millions of files between storage tiers would be impossible. Automation is a necessity for utilizing multi-tier storage effectively. The more files an enterprise has, and the more active they are, the more of a necessity automated placement becomes.

The Dynamic Storage Tiering (DST) facility, available with Version 5 of the Storage Foundation, exploits multi-tier online storage effectively without administrative overhead. The DST facility has two parts:

- The ability to distribute a single file system ("name space") across multiple VxVM volumes with different properties
- Automatic policy-based placement and relocation of files among a file system's volume set

The individual volumes used by a VxFS multi-volume file system are transparent to applications. But VxFS itself remains aware of each volume's tier classification, and implements pre-defined policies that dynamically control the type of device on which each file is stored.

VxFS administrators define policies that automatically control both initial file location and the circumstances under which VxFS relocates existing files. Policies consist of rules that restrict files' locations to designated storage tiers. Policy rules cause files to be created and extended within specified tiers, and to be relocated to other tiers when they meet certain qualifications such as size, I/O activity, and location within the name space.

Conclusion: Storage Foundation utilizes multiple tiers of online storage effectively by automatically creating each file on the "right" type of storage, and moving it to its new "right" type of storage when conditions around it change, all without administrative intervention.

Virtualization of storage across the storage network

Starting with the first RAID-capable disk arrays of the early 1990s, the storage presented to enterprise applications has increasingly become virtualized. Today, most file systems and database management systems store their data not directly on disk drives, but on disk drive-like virtual devices. The virtual devices consist of one or more disk drives plus a layer of software that coordinates the drives' activities and presents disk drive-like virtual devices to file systems, database management systems, and storage utilities.

Virtual storage devices are functionally equivalent to disk drives as far as reading and writing data are concerned, but they offer superior I/O performance, device availability, data reliability, and function compared to the disk drives of which they consist. As storage has moved out of the server and onto the network, virtualization technology has evolved to encompass logical connectivity of storage devices to systems as well.

Early implementations of the control software for storage virtualization were done in disk array firmware and in server-based volume managers like VxVM. In recent years, vendors of storage network switches and directors have added storage virtualization capabilities to their devices as well. The logical location of virtualization software in the data center determines the scope over which it can operate as well as the application and database servers to which it can present the storage it virtualizes. Table 2-3 summarizes the scope of virtualization for disk arrays, storage network switches, and servers.

Table 2-3 Scope of storage virtualization

Virtualization location	Properties
Disk array firmware	Disk drives: Can virtualize disk drives within the array, but has no ability to control drives in other arrays. Hosts: Can present virtual devices to hosts with physical and logical connectivity to the array's SAN ports.
Storage network switch firmware	Disk drives: Can virtualize devices presented to the switch. These may include both disk drives and LUNs that have already been virtualized by disk array firmware. Hosts: Can present its virtual devices to hosts with physical and logical connectivity to its SAN ports.
Application or database server software like VxVM	Disk drives: Can virtualize disk drives and LUNs to whose storage network ports it has physical and logical connectivity through the storage network. Hosts: Can present virtual devices to applications running on the application or database server, but not to other applications on other servers.

Studying Table 2-3, it becomes obvious that none of the conventional loci of storage virtualization operates on a global scale, that is, none can virtualize an arbitrary pool of a data center's storage devices and present virtual devices to an arbitrary collection of computers. In data centers with only a few servers, with storage either directly attached or configured statically, the limited scope of virtualization is of minor concern. But as enterprises deploy larger numbers of smaller blade servers, and storage redeployments become a daily occurrence, the lack of a larger vantage point from which to manage storage increasingly limits the ability to utilize storage assets effectively.

Responding to this need for a larger scope of control over data center storage, Version 5 of the Storage Foundation enhances volume manager capabilities to provide centrally controlled virtualization of pools of storage resources that are accessible by groups of hosts. Using the new Storage Foundation Volume Server capability, arbitrary sets of hosts attached to a storage network can share access to the same pool of VxVM disk groups, no matter what type of UNIX platform they run. With Volume Server, hosts write and read data directly to and from storage devices, but configuration and state management is done by highly-available management servers that act on behalf of the entire set of hosts.

Administrators manage storage resource pools for groups of hosts from a single point, with visibility to all resources and storage consumers.

Conclusion: With the Storage Foundation Volume Server facility, storage resource sharing and serial data sharing between arbitrary groups of UNIX hosts of all supported types becomes fast and seamless.

Chapter 3

A closer look at the Storage Foundation core: the VxVM Volume Manager

This chapter includes the following topics:

- Why Storage Foundation?
- The VxVM volume manager
- New in the Storage Foundation: multi-host coordinated storage management

Why Storage Foundation?

The core components of the Storage Foundation, the VxVM volume manager and the VxFS file system, occupy a position at the heart of the data center software stack. So fundamental are host-based storage virtualization and file organization and management to enterprise computing that UNIX and Linux operating systems include native virtualizers and file systems. This raises the question of whether investment in the Storage Foundation is justifiable, or, put another way, whether UNIX and Linux native file systems and volume managers are good enough to meet basic enterprise needs.

For most enterprises, the answer to this question is a strong affirmative. Storage Foundation capabilities go well beyond those offered by common built-in virtualizers and file systems. The value that the Storage Foundation adds to a data center above and beyond operating systems' native components falls into three basic categories:

- Advanced function that makes Storage Foundation scale to manage thousands of storage devices and tens of millions of files.

- Platform support that makes it possible to manage storage and data for all of a data center's UNIX and Linux platforms with a single set of procedures controlled from a single management console.
- Integration that makes Storage Foundation I/O performance, data availability, and storage asset management easily accessible to other software infrastructure components such as cluster and storage network managers, as well as major database management systems and applications.

A more detailed understanding of how the Storage Foundation delivers its value requires a closer look at both the nature of storage virtualization and how the core Storage Foundation components implement their functions.

Storage virtualization

In information technology, virtualization usually means combining readily available physical components to produce the behavior of a component or service that is difficult (or impossible) to obtain. For example, disks with 1,000,000,000 hour mean time to data loss and disks capable of executing 2,500 I/O requests per second are impossible to build, or at least prohibitively expensive to obtain. But virtual disks with these properties can be created easily by mirroring identical data on two or more disks and striping block addresses across a dozen or more disks respectively.

Storage devices are virtualized by software that manages one or more physical devices, mapping client read and write requests to virtual storage to commands to the managed devices. Virtualization has two parts:

- Algorithms that determine how client I/O requests map to I/O operations on disks or disk array LUNs.
- Configuration information that drives the algorithms. Configuration information defines which physical devices comprise which parts of virtual devices, and the types of algorithms used to access them.

For example, the algorithm for mirrored virtual devices is to execute each client write request on all devices and to choose one device to execute each client read request. For striped virtual devices, the algorithm converts virtual device block addresses into block addresses on one or more physical devices and executes client read and write requests by issuing commands to the selected devices.

Algorithms are executable code that loads each time a virtualizer starts to execute. In this sense, they are volatile—every time a virtualizer restarts, a new copy of its algorithms is loaded. If the storage device containing virtualization software is destroyed, the software can be reinstalled on a replacement device.

Configuration information, on the other hand, must be persistent. It is the only way a virtualizer has of determining which physical devices comprise which parts of which virtual devices so that it can execute its algorithms correctly. Not only must virtual storage configuration information persist across system restarts, it must persist across storage device failure and replacement. In a sense, virtual storage configuration information is the most valuable data an enterprise has. It is the key by which application data is located. If virtual storage configuration information is lost, an enterprise is in the frustrating position of knowing that its important data is physically intact on functioning devices that are under its control, but being utterly unable to locate and access it.

The VxVM volume manager

The VxVM volume manager is a host-based storage virtualization tool for the Solaris, HP-UX, AIX, Red Hat Linux, and SuSe Linux platforms. VxVM operates above the hardware device driver layer in the data access software stack, as Figure 3-1 illustrates. Disk and I/O adapter drivers are typically supplied as part of an operating system, or by the vendors of storage and I/O adapter hardware. Because it is essentially a client of any and all disk storage drivers that are installed in a system, VxVM can virtualize any disk storage device that an operating system supports. For virtualization purposes, VxVM treats all disk drives and disk array LUNs presented to it through drivers identically as generic VxVM disk objects.

The ability to virtualize all types of storage is a key advantage in making a data center storage strategy independent of hardware vendors. When new types of devices are introduced, or old ones are retired, no change in virtualization strategy is required. If the new devices are roughly equivalent to the old ones in terms of I/O performance and data protection, they can be substituted for the old devices and instantly recognized and managed by VxVM.

Figure 3-1 VxVM's position in the data access software stack

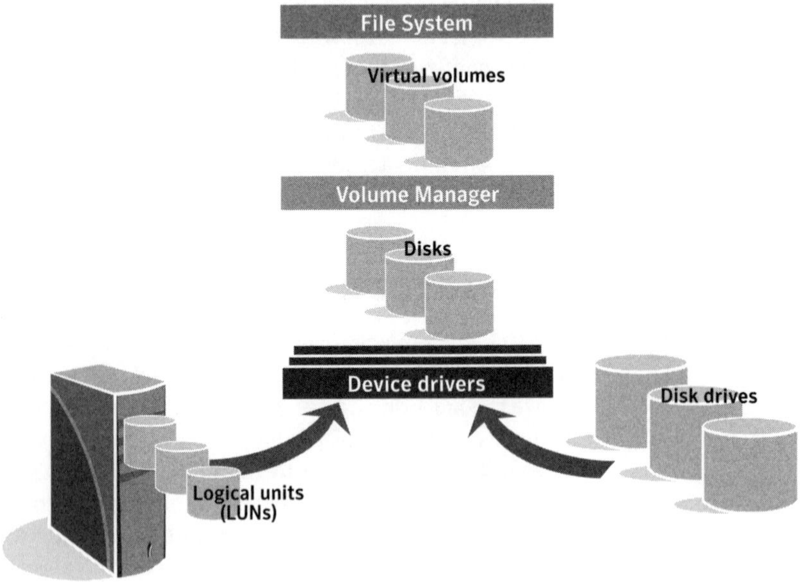

VxVM transactions

VxVM treats all disk drives and disk array LUNs visible to it through the driver stack identically as abstract disk objects, which it organizes into disk groups. All VxVM virtualization and other management operations occur within the confines of a disk group. For example, a disk in one disk group is never mirrored with a disk in another group.

The disk group organization makes storage management more reliable, particularly for large numbers of storage devices in complex networks connected to many hosts. For example, to transfer control of a set of disks from one application server to another, an administrator would split the disks from their disk group, form a separate group, deport the new group from the controlling server, and import it on the target server. If anything were to go wrong during this sequence of steps, disks could be left in indeterminate states, belonging to either one disk group or another, or worse, to both.

VxVM makes these and other management operations like them reliable by performing them as transactions. In information technology, the term "transaction" has a well-defined meaning that is often summed up in the phrase "ACID properties." The ACID properties of digital transactions are:

- Atomicity, meaning that at the end of a transaction, either all the primitive operations that comprise it have executed to completion, or they have been reversed so that the effect on the system is as though the transaction had never occurred
- Consistency, meaning that a transaction transforms a system from one valid state to another (primarily a property of application correctness)
- Isolation, meaning that no matter how many transactions are executing concurrently, each behaves as though it were the only one running in the system
- Durability, meaning that when a transaction signals that it is complete, its results persist, even if the system on which it is running fails immediately after the completion signal is given

VxVM transactions manage disks, disk configurations, and disk content layout. For example, allocating part of a disk's capacity for a volume, combining two disks into a mirrored volume, and adding a disk to a striped volume are all processed as transactions. Because VxVM management operations are transactional, administrators need not concern themselves with recovering from failures that occur in mid-operation; VxVM makes sure that management operations either complete or are backed out—disks and other objects are never lost or left under the apparent control of two servers.

Private regions

VxVM disk groups are self-describing, meaning that the disks in a group contain information about group membership, volumes, and other VxVM objects. As Figure 3-2 illustrates, VxVM divides the total storage capacity of each disk it manages into a small (a few megabytes) private region in which it stores its metadata, and a much larger data storage region that it makes available for application use.

Figure 3-2 VxVM private and public regions

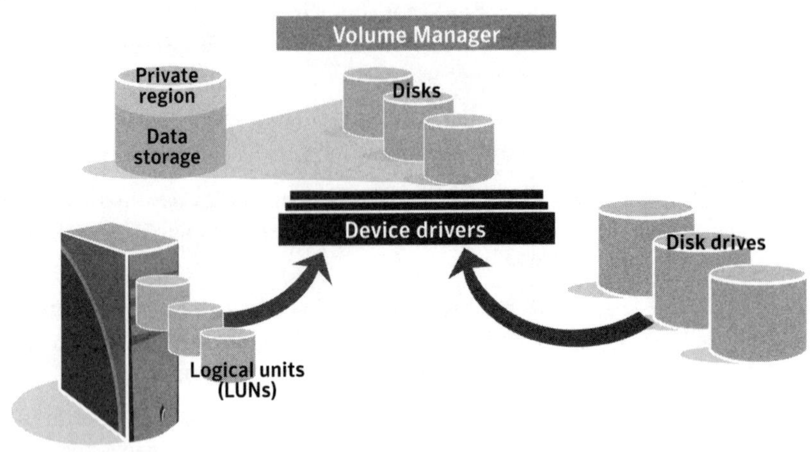

Taken together, the private regions of the disks in a disk group describe the complete configuration of the group. Each disk's private region contains basic facts about the disk group as a whole, a description of the volumes and other VxVM objects of which the disk is a part, and redundant copies of information about other disks in the group. All information about a disk group is stored in two or more disks' private regions so that the durability property of VxVM transactions can be guaranteed—even if one or more disks fails, VxVM can use metadata from the private regions of the remaining disks in the group to reconstruct the group's volume configuration.

VxVM achieves the remaining transactional properties, atomicity, consistency, and isolation through a combination of carefully sequenced private region updates and its own resource locking mechanism. The result is a repository of virtual storage configuration information that is robust, both in the sense of being proof against multiple storage device failures and in the sense of being updated in such a way that it can be recovered to a correct starting point if a system fails at any point during an update. Because VxVM disks are self-describing, configuration information travels with them, so that, for example, when control of a disk group containing striped or mirrored volumes is transferred from one server to another, the configuration of the volumes and the user data on them survives the transfer intact.

VxVM object naming

UNIX systems discover the storage devices connected to them when they start up by probing I/O bus addresses, or by querying storage network name servers. Each discovered device is given a name that is related to the I/O bus adapter on which it is discovered, or to its worldwide storage network name. The names become part of the operating system's device tree, and are used in management operations such as virtual volume and file system creation.

While operating system device naming schemes guarantee that every device visible to a system is named uniquely, the names they produce have two shortcomings:

- They are difficult for human administrators to use on a daily basis, because they have no relationship to business purpose.
- They fail to distinguish between separate devices and a single device with two or more connections to the system.

VxVM's user-friendly device naming capability overcomes the first of these shortcomings. The second is overcome by the Dynamic Multi-pathing (DMP) capability discussed in Chapter 5.

For a system with only a few storage devices connected to it, device naming is simple. Storage device configurations change infrequently, so administrators naturally come to memorize device names and their relationships to other parts of the IT operation during the course of their daily work. It is easy to remember that the disk or LUN called `/dev/dsk/c0t0d1s0` contains the file system for the accounts payable application. But as systems are reconfigured, and as more systems and more disk arrays are installed in a data center, relationships change, and it quickly becomes impossible to hold the storage configuration in one person's memory. As a data center acquires more administrators, the problem is compounded because the administrators must coordinate their every action so that each administrator's mental picture of the data center's storage is the same as all others.

Storage virtualization compounds the difficulty further by adding more objects—virtual volumes and the storage components that comprise them—whose names must be specified correctly in management operations.

VxVM's object naming scheme mitigates the problem of quick, reliable human identification of devices from their names. The VxVM naming scheme has three important aspects that simplify human recognition and management of storage objects:

- Default object names that correlate with other VxVM objects
- User-assignable object names

- Enclosure-based naming of VxVM disk objects

The first two columns of the display in Dialog 3-1 which designate the VxVM object type and object name respectively, illustrate the first two of these three aspects of the VxVM object naming scheme.

Dialog 3-1 VxVM object naming

```
[1]  # vxassist -g testdg make appvol 100m nmirror=2
[2]  # vxprint
[3]  Disk group: testdg
[4]  TY NAME         ASSOC        KSTATE   LENGTH   PLOFFS   STATE    TUTIL0  PUTIL0
[5]  dg testdg       testdg       -        -        -        -        -       -
[6]  dm c3t1d0s2     c3t1d0s2     -        71680896 -        -        -       -
[7]  dm c3t2d0s2     c3t2d0s2     -        71680896 -        -        -       -
[8]  v  appvol       fsgen        ENABLED  204800   -        ACTIVE   -       -
[9]  pl appvol-01    appvol       ENABLED  204800   -        ACTIVE   -       -
[10] sd c3t1d0s2-01  appvol-01    ENABLED  204800   0        -        -       -
[11] pl appvol-02    appvol       ENABLED  204800   -        ACTIVE   -       -
[12] sd c3t2d0s2-01  appvol-02    ENABLED  204800   0        -        -       -
```

Lines `[6]`-`[7]` in Dialog 1 represent two `dm` (disk media) objects. These are disk drives or disk array LUNs that have been placed under VxVM control. The names by which the disks are addressed in VxVM administrative commands, for example, `c3t1d0s2`, appear in the second column of the display. The third column of the display represents an object with which the VxVM object is associated, in this case, the operating system's name for the device. VxVM has set the names by which it recognizes the devices to be identical to those assigned by the operating system. If for some administrative reason it were more appropriate to give VxVM disk objects other names, that is also possible.

Line `[8]` represents a VxVM virtual volume (object type `v`) that is presented to clients. The `vxassist` command in line `[1]` of the Dialog creates the volume, which is mirrored, and names it `appvol` for administrative convenience. A VxVM volume consists of one or more objects called plexes (object type `pl`), which in turn consist of subdisks (object type `sd`). Lines `[9]` and `[11]` illustrate that the plex objects, which are created automatically by VxVM during the course of volume creation, are named `appvol-01` and `appvol-02`, and are thus immediately identifiable as being associated with the `appvol` volume. Lines `[10]` and `[12]` represent subdisk objects `c3t1d0s2-01` and `c3t2d0s2-01`, which VxVM names by default based on the disk objects on which they reside. The `ASSOC` column of the display indicates that these subdisks are associated with their respective plex objects.

The similar (abbreviated) display of the structure of a striped volume in Dialog 3-2 illustrates the third aspect of VxVM object naming—enclosure-based names. When enclosure-based naming is in effect, VxVM gives all LUNs that report a particular array type (`SHARK0` in this case) disk media names that identify the enclosure that houses them (SHARK0_26 and SHARK0_27 in Dialog 3-2). Enclosure-based names are generated by array model-specific VxVM modules called Array Support Modules (ASMs).

With enclosure-based naming, physical locations of LUNs are thus instantly identifiable. If application or business oriented names are more appropriate, VxVM can substitute a user-defined enclosure name for that reported by the array, and disks are named according to the substitute name.

Dialog 3-2 VxVM enclosure-based naming

```
[1] Disk group: tcrundg
[2] dg tcrundg       default      default  16000     140131242.57.vm280r1.veritas.com
[3] dm IBM_SHARK0_26 IBM_SHARK0_26 auto    65536     1883008  -
[4] dm IBM_SHARK0_27 IBM_SHARK0_27 auto    2048      1946496  -
[5] v  appvol        -            ENABLED  ACTIVE    20480    SELECT     appvol-01 gen
[6] pl appvol-01     appvol       ENABLED  ACTIVE    20480    STRIPE     2/128     RW
[7] sd IBM_SHARK0_26-01 appvol-01 IBM_SHARK0_26 0   10240    0/0        IBM_SHARK0_26 ENA
[8] sd IBM_SHARK0_27-01 appvol-01 IBM_SHARK0_27 0   10240    1/0        IBM_SHARK0_27 ENA
```

As these simple examples illustrate, VxVM automates default object naming so that related objects can easily be correlated with each other. Enclosure-based names automatically correlate LUNs with the disk array enclosures that present them. Moreover, VxVM object names are completely at administrator discretion. Administrators can design storage naming schemes to meet enterprise requirements, be they application-oriented, data center layout-oriented, or designed for some other business purpose.

Multipath access to storage

As data centers have evolved from configuring storage for each individual server, and adopted the pooled storage concept enabled by storage networks, the storage network itself has become an important factor in delivering high data and application availability. Not only must virtual storage devices be robust, but the ability to access the physical devices that comprise them must be protected against network failures as well.

The primary mechanism for making connections between hosts and storage devices failure-tolerant is to provide multiple paths between the two. If one path fails, communications between host and device can continue using an alternate path.

Most data managers and storage utilities equate a single network storage address with a single device. In order to make it possible to use these software components with devices to which there are multiple access paths, the paths to the devices are virtualized—storage applications running in hosts address pseudo-devices. A layer of host software routes all I/O requests to a given device along one or more of the access paths, and tracks outstanding requests until their execution is complete.

The most failure tolerant form of multipath access is to configure two completely separate physical networks, or fabrics, and connect both host server and storage device to both fabrics, as Figure 3-3 illustrates.

Figure 3-3 Multiple paths to networked storage devices

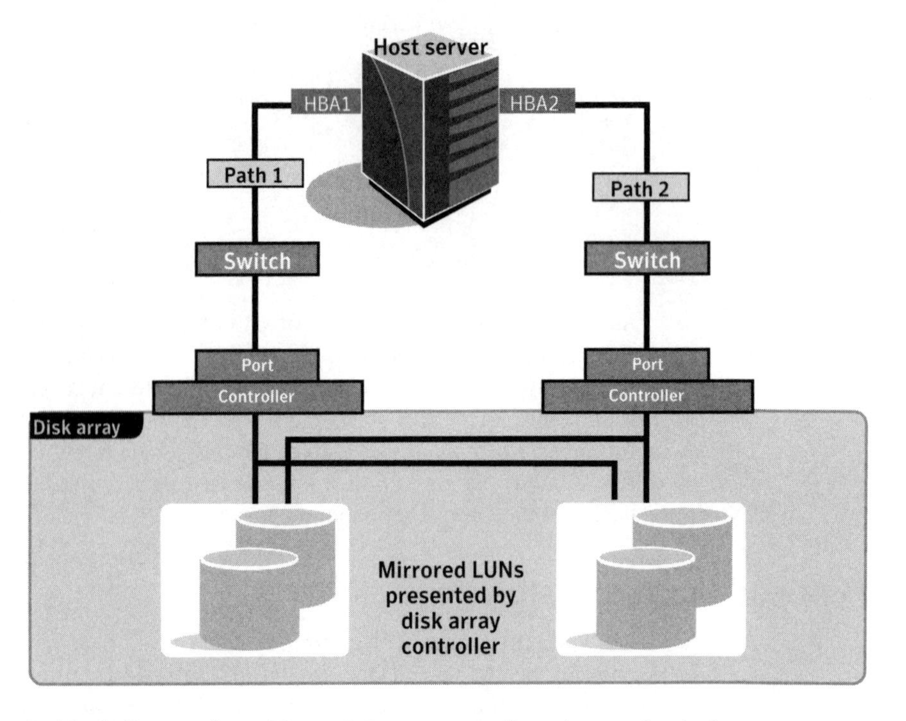

In block diagram form, Figure 3-3 represents the primary physical components in the path between server and storage devices (in this case, mirrored devices virtualized by disk array firmware.

The two blocks labeled `switch` in Figure 3-3 represent separate storage network fabrics with no shared components except the end point host server and disk array memory systems. Separate host bus adapters (HBAs), cables, disk controllers and disk controller ports provide two completely independent paths between host server and virtual devices. Any single component in either path can fail without interrupting the connection between host server and data, provided that:

- The host server recognizes that there are two paths between it and the storage devices.

- The host server's I/O software stack is able to re-channel requests made to the failed path to the alternate path so that applications' access to data is uninterrupted.

VxVM's Dynamic Multi-pathing (DMP) feature fulfills both of these requirements. DMP builds on basic operating system device discovery to recognize multiple paths to the same disk drive or disk array LUN. If the path to a device fails for any reason, DMP re-routes requests to an alternate path. In most cases, re-routing is transparent to applications. For so-called active-passive disk arrays that require specific action to communicate with a device on an alternate path, DMP performs the required actions.

Figure 3-4 Dynamic multi-pathing in the storage I/O stack

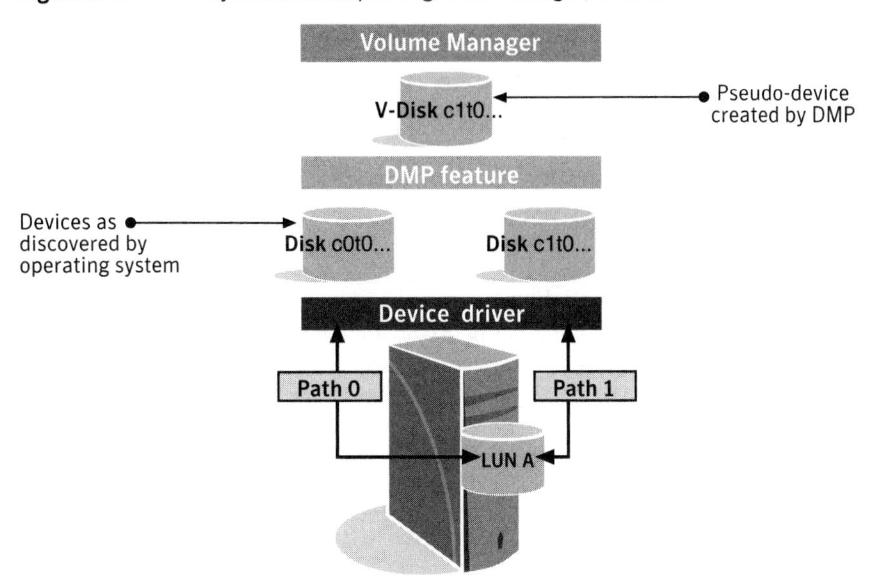

Figure 3-4 illustrates that DMP occupies a position below the VxVM virtualization layer in the I/O stack. During its discovery phase, which occurs at system startup, and may also occur on demand, DMP queries similar devices to determine whether they are actually different devices, or the same device presented to the operating system through two host bus adapters. For each device to which it detects multiple paths, DMP creates a pseudo-device data structure in the operating system.

VxVM's virtualization layer virtualizes (mirrors, stripes, and so forth) the pseudo-devices presented by DMP. Every I/O request issued to a driver by VxVM passes through the DMP layer, which routes it on an I/O path to a device, and tracks its progress so that VxVM I/O requests are not lost in the system.

If a path to an I/O device fails, DMP simply re-routes outstanding and future requests to another path, performing any disk array-specific actions required to effect path failover.

A secondary benefit of DMP is the ability to use two or more paths to a device concurrently to increase throughput. This feature is especially valuable with enterprise-class disk arrays with large cache memories. For certain types of applications, sizable percentages of I/O requests are satisfied by referencing disk array cache. Because there are no seeking or rotational delays for these requests, data transfer is the factor that limits I/O performance. If a disk array supports concurrent access to its LUNs on two or more paths, DMP can route each VxVM I/O request to the least busy path for improved overall throughput. DMP includes several algorithms for balancing I/O load across multiple paths.

The primary benefit of DMP is an increase in data availability at the server level because it makes access to storage devices tolerant of I/O path failure. A secondary benefit is improved I/O performance when used with disk arrays that can support concurrent access on multiple I/O paths to the LUNs they present.

Online reconfiguration

As data centers grow in size and complexity, and as the velocity of change in digital data processing increases, server and storage reconfiguration becomes a fact of daily life. Application data outgrow allocated storage capacity; data sets' value to their owners increase, requiring greater protection; systems with an excess of storage capacity donate part of it to other systems with too little.

Whatever the reason, reconfiguration spells "downtime" for applications, a word that is increasingly becoming an anathema to administrators required to keep their applications up and running around the clock. Taking a large file system or database out of service so it can be backed up and restored to a larger device is often intolerable from a business standpoint. Even the time required to copy a data set from non-redundant devices directly to mirrored ones may impact operations adversely.

VxVM's architecture eliminates or at least mitigates many of these storage reconfiguration issues by making it possible to perform them while data is online and in use by applications. Volumes can be resized, both to greater capacity, when an application needs it, and to lesser capacity, when unused storage must be redeployed to other hosts.

Volume configurations can be changed while the volumes are in use by applications. Mirrors can be added or removed. The number of columns in a striped volume can be increased or decreased, again, while data on the volumes is being used by applications. Even parity RAID volumes can be reconfigured by the addition of columns.

VxVM can relocate a single mirror or column of a striped volume from one disk or LUN to another. This feature is useful when potential disk failure is suspected—data can be moved from the failing disk to an alternate one while it is in use. It is also useful for migrating data from older devices to newer ones.

VxVM performs all of these reconfiguration operations in the background, using I/O capacity that is not being used by applications. But all data reconfiguration operations entail significant amounts of I/O, so it is prudent to schedule them for periods when production applications are not at peak load. What VxVM online reconfiguration does accomplish is the elimination of downtime—applications can be fully functional while reconfiguration is going on, even if not at peak performance. Thus, online reconfiguration turns a hard boundary into a soft one. Instead of requiring that an application be out of service for as long as it takes to reconfigure its storage, VxVM only requires that reconfiguration be scheduled at a time when any potential performance degradation can be tolerated from a business standpoint.

Snapshots

Applications are increasingly required to operate around the clock. From early adopters like air traffic control, to business-to-business functions like funds transfer, to web retail applications, what started as a convenience has become an imperative. An information service that isn't available around the clock is simply not viable. Somewhere, there is a competing service that is continuously available.

But at the same time, enterprises are becoming increasingly dependent on their digital information to operate. It is a rare enterprise, no matter how small, that can function without its computer systems and digital information. Thus, enterprises must preserve and protect their digital data, just as they preserve and protect cash, capital equipment, and other valuable assets.

These two trends conflict with each other. One the one hand, data must be available for use around the clock. On the other, it must remain unmodified long enough for copies to be made to protect it against destruction.

VxVM snapshots that capture split-second images of large data sets, much as photographic snapshots capture images of physical action, help resolve this conflict. A VxVM snapshot of a large data set can be backed up or otherwise processed while the data itself continues to be processed by production applications.

VxVM supports both full-copy and space-saving allocate-on-write snapshots. A full-copy snapshot is a bit-for-bit copy of a volume, occupying as much storage capacity as the volume itself. Full-copy snapshots have the advantage that the storage devices they occupy can be moved to other hosts, so processing them does not detract from the resources available to production applications. They have the disadvantage that initial creation takes a long time, because every bit of the data set whose snapshot is being taken must be copied to the snapshot volume.

Space-saving snapshots are virtual snapshots of volumes. Physically, a space-saving snapshot includes only the prior images of data that is modified after snapshot creation. Storage capacity for the prior images is allocated when they are updated by applications. Space-saving snapshots are presented as complete data sets, but they satisfy read requests for unmodified data by referring to the original image. For this reason, they cannot be moved off-host to another computer for auxiliary processing.

Space-saving snapshots use storage capacity very economically, especially for large data sets with low rates of change—they consume storage capacity in proportion to the amount of data modified during their lifetimes rather than in proportion to the size of the data set. Thus, it is feasible to take frequent space-saving snapshots so that data sets can be quickly restored to former states (recovery points) if they become corrupted.

The VxVM FastResync™ feature greatly enhances the usability of both full-copy and space-saving snapshots in repetitive applications and for recovering from application-caused data corruption. VxVM maintains Data Change Logs (DCLs) that track changes both for active snapshots and for the volumes whose snapshots they represent. Using DCLs as guides, VxVM can quickly restore a corrupted volume to a prior state by overwriting changed blocks with the contents of their prior images from a snapshot. Similarly, a snapshot whose useful life is over can be updated to a more recent one by overwriting changed blocks from the original volume to it. Thus, for example, a full-copy snapshot can be taken off-host for backup, and after the backup is complete, be brought back on-host updated to the current state of its original volume by copying changed data to it, and taken off-host again for the next backup cycle.

VxVM snapshots can dramatically increase information service uptime by making it possible to capture instantaneous states of large data sets that can be backed up or analyzed while production applications continue to process live data. Snapshots can be used to recover from corruption of production data by restoring data to a state it was in at some point prior to the occurrence of the corruption. FastResync™ technology increases the utility of snapshots by reducing the amount of copying required for both the restoration of prior volume states and the refreshing of snapshots to the minimum possible.

Storage provisioning

Storage provisioning is yet another administrative complexity that results from the migration of data center storage out of the server and onto the network. Simply put, storage provisioning is the process of configuring virtual storage capacity from physical devices and placing that virtual capacity under the control of one or more application or database servers.

In a data center in which servers use directly attached storage (DAS), storage provisioning is relatively simple. Each storage device is permanently associated with one server. The only provisioning action required is to configure virtual devices appropriately—to organize disk drives or disk array LUNs into mirrored, striped, or other types of virtual volumes.

When storage devices are connected to a network and accessible by all servers, however, storage provisioning becomes more complex. From a pool of unallocated disk drives and LUNs, an administrator must select appropriate physical devices, place them under control of one server or cluster, and configure them as volumes that can be used by applications. In a data center with dozens or hundreds of servers, and potentially thousands of disk drives and LUNs, keeping track of what physical devices are available for provisioning and how allocated devices are configured becomes difficult if not impossible to do in a timely and error-free manner.

Over its history, VxVM's storage provisioning capabilities have evolved in parallel with the complexity and connectivity of the data center environments in which it is used. VxVM's provisioning capabilities can best be appreciated with an understanding of the internal structure of VxVM volumes. Figure 3-5 represents the primary VxVM objects and how they are used to construct the virtual volumes that are presented to applications.

Figure 3-5 VxVM objects

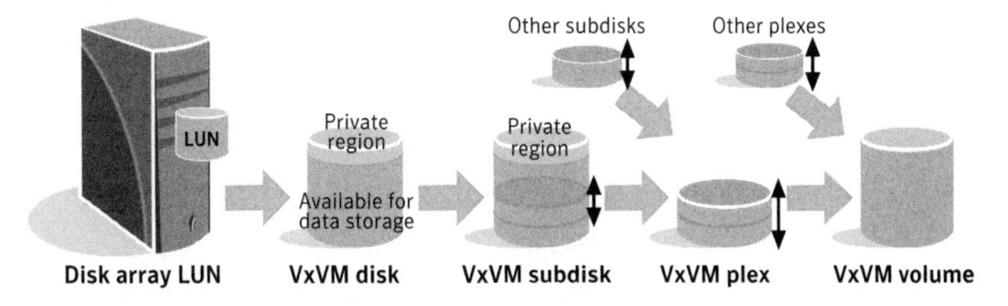

Starting from the left side of Figure 3-5, VxVM recognizes the LUNs presented to hosts by disk arrays (or disk drives presented directly in smaller systems). When VxVM takes control of a LUN or disk drive, it divides the block address space into two contiguous ranges called the private and public regions respectively. VxVM stores its own metadata in the small private region; the far larger public region is available for assembly into higher level objects that are ultimately used for user data storage. Such a LUN or disk drive controlled by VxVM is called simply a disk.

The public region of a VxVM disk can be subdivided into ranges of consecutive block addresses called subdisks. Subdisks are the underpinning that makes it possible to divide the capacity of a very large disk into smaller units for presentation to applications as volumes, or alternatively, to distribute the capacity of a single volume across multiple physical resources to improve I/O performance.

One or more subdisks can be organized into a single block address range called a plex. While it is presented upward as a single block address range, the blocks that comprise a plex may be distributed across a number of disk array LUNs or disk drives.

Finally, one or more plexes can be organized into a volume, which is the unit of virtual storage on which file systems are formatted and presented for use by applications.

This four-level object hierarchy of disk, subdisk, plex, and volume provides the administrator with precise control over storage resource allocation. For example, an administrator can define subdisks using capacity on four different VxVM disks representing pairs of LUNs presented by two different disk arrays. The two pairs of subdisks can be made into striped plexes, which in turn can be mirrored with each other and presented as a volume. Figure 3-6 illustrates this construction.

Figure 3-6 Constructing a VxVM volume: an example

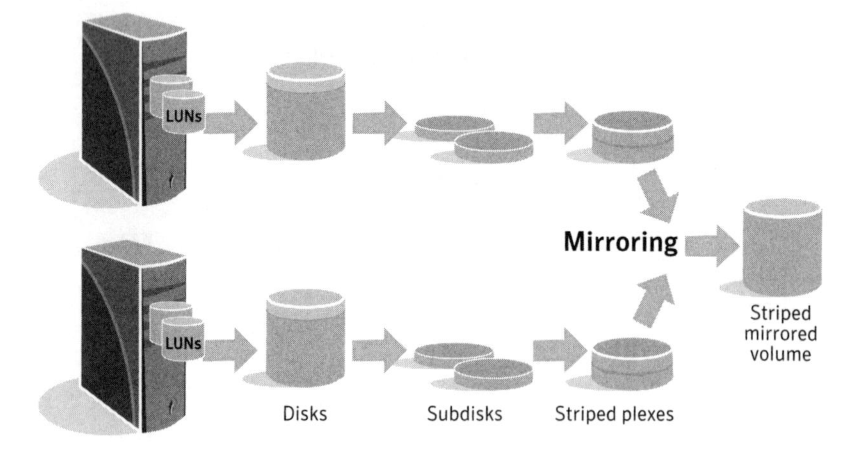

The resulting volume has two important desirable characteristics:

- Striping tends to balance I/O load across the two subdisks of each plex.
- Mirroring protects data on the volume against loss due to the failure of any one of the four disks that contribute capacity to it.

Subdisks, plexes, and volumes can all be constructed using the VxVM `vxmake` console commands or the Veritas Enterprise Administrator graphical interface. This is referred to as the advanced approach to volume management. With the advanced approach, a system administrator is responsible for determining the appropriate storage layout, for example, ensuring that the subdisks that will comprise a striped plex are presented on different ports of the same disk array, and that the two plexes consist of storage presented by different disk arrays.

While working directly with VxVM subdisks and plexes gives administrators precise control over volume configuration, the advanced approach has an important shortcoming that becomes apparent as a data center grows and becomes more complex. Administrators who manage each basic VxVM object directly must keep track of each subdisk and plex throughout its life, and, more importantly, must allocate every new or reconfigured volume so that it meets the enterprise's business intent for data sets.

For example, if enterprise policy dictates that every critical data set must be stored on volumes that are mirrored on LUNs presented by different disk arrays, it is up to the administrator to identify and configure appropriate LUNs every time users require a new volume. Similarly, if enterprise policy dictates that critical datasets must be accessible on at least two I/O paths, it is the administrators' responsibility to ensure that every new volume is configured from VxVM disks that are reachable on at least two paths.

With disk arrays capable of presenting a thousand or more LUNs, keeping track of individual disks, subdisks and plexes is clearly impractical. More importantly, individually configuring thousands of volumes from their basic VxVM components is almost guaranteed to result in configuration errors, or at a minimum, in enterprise data management policies not being followed.

Recognizing that data center growth, and in particular, online storage growth, was routinely creating situations in which the sheer amount of online storage made management difficult and error-prone, Veritas introduced assisted volume configuration with Version 2 of the Storage Foundation in 1994. Administrators can use assisted volume configuration to create, reconfigure and resize volumes through the `vxassist` console command as well as through the Veritas Enterprise Administrator (VEA) graphical console. Assisted volume configuration simplifies online storage management in three ways:

- It encapsulates the VxVM operations that manipulate basic objects so that administrators deal explicitly only with volumes.

- It promotes configuration consistency by storing common installation default parameters such as stripe width and mirror count in a file, and using them as default values when executing management commands.
- It relieves administrators of the responsibility of tracking disk usage by choosing the disks from which to create, expand, or reconfigure a volume wherever possible.

Thus, for example, creating the mirrored striped volume shown in Figure 3-6 using the advanced configuration technique would require that an administrator choose two pairs of LUNs presented by the two disk arrays and represented as VxVM disks, and issue `vxmake` commands to create the subdisks, plexes, and finally the volume. Assuming that defaults have been set to create mirrored striped volumes, using assisted volume configuration reduces the administrative acts to create this volume to the single command shown in line `[1]` of Dialog 3-3.

Dialog 3-3 Using vxassist to create volumes

```
[1] # vxassist -g diskgroupA make volume01 100g
[2] # vxassist -g diskgroupA make volume02 100g diskgroupA01 diskgroupA02
[3] # vxassist -g diskgroupA make volume03 100g !diskgroupA03 !ctlr:c2
[4] # vxassist -g diskgroupA make volume04 maxsize layout=raid5
```

The `vxassist` command simplifies volume creation to the greatest extent possible, while still providing the flexibility for administrators to configure storage to meet individual requirements. For example, line `[2]` of Dialog 3-3 shows how an administrator can specify the VxVM disks on which a volume should be created. Line `[3]` illustrates how specific disks (`diskgroupA03`), and disks connected to specific controllers (`ctlr:c2`) can be excluded from being part of a volume. Line `[4]` shows how the default volume type (striped mirrored) can be overridden by specifying `layout=raid5`, and also how the maximum available capacity in the disk group can be incorporated into the volume by specifying `maxsize` rather than a numeric value. Dialog 3-3 illustrates basic examples of `vxassist`; many other options are available to meet the goals of simplicity and flexibility.

In all of the examples in Dialog 3-3, VxVM creates the basic subdisk and plex objects automatically, choosing appropriate locations for them within the constraints specified. For example, when the `vxassist` command is used to create a mirrored striped volume, VxVM ensures that each column of the stripes is located on a different disk, and that the mirrored plexes do not have any disks in common. If possible, it allocates the low-level objects for a volume to disks connected to different host bus adapters to minimize I/O contention for the volume.

With assisted volume configuration, administrators are relieved of most of the necessity for inventorying storage capacity and allocation, as well as the necessity of using low-level VxVM commands to create VxVM objects below the volume level.

This form of the `vxassist` command greatly simplifies virtual volume administration, and perhaps more importantly, reduces the potential for configuration errors. As disk arrays have become more complex, however, and as users have become more sophisticated about how they configure and account for their online storage, the need for even more sophisticated virtual storage configuration has become apparent. For example:

- Larger data centers often have two or more enterprise-class disk arrays, and define policies that mirror critical data on LUNs in separate arrays.
- The virtualization performed by disk arrays must be coordinated in some way with VxVM virtualization. For example, mirrored LUNs presented by a disk array may not need to be mirrored again by VxVM.
- As disk array capabilities have become more sophisticated, purely hierarchical relationships such as that between LUNs and controller ports on the storage network are no longer valid.
- As storage networks have grown and become more complex, ensuring that all components of automatically-configured volumes are reachable on two or more independent paths has become a priority.
- IT service providers that have service level agreements with their user organizations often require that certain physical storage capacity be allocated only to certain users.

To meet the need for more general forms of automated volume configuration, Version 4 of the Storage Foundation introduced the Intelligent Storage Provisioning facility. Intelligent Storage Provisioning makes it possible to configure virtual volumes based on templates that describe required properties in a very general way. For example, a template may specify that mirrored volumes can be mirrored either by VxVM or by the disk arrays that present the underlying VxVM disks. Alternatively, a template may specify that mirrored volumes must consist of mirrors in two different disk array enclosures.

Equally important, with Intelligent Storage Provisioning, arbitrary name-value pairs called attributes may be assigned to disks. These attributes are entirely user-determined—they can be used to represent any desired business property. For example, if a data center's storage is in several disk arrays split between two buildings on a campus, attributes can be used to signify the building location of individual LUNs. Templates can then be defined to cause mirrored volumes to be either co-located or split between the two buildings. Alternatively, attributes can signify a business function for which storage is reserved, such as engineering, sales, or accounting. Templates can then be defined for engineering volumes, sales volumes, and accounting volumes, each specifying that it must be allocated from storage devices with the corresponding attribute.

Version 5 of the Storage Foundation links Intelligent Storage Provisioning with assisted volume configuration. Beginning with Version 5, it is possible to specify disk attributes in `vxassist` commands, making it possible to constrain volumes to be created from disks with specified attributes or conversely. Dialog 3-4 illustrates how user-defined configurations can be created and modified quickly and easily, while still preserving an enterprise's intent for its storage.

Dialog 3-4 Using vxassist combined with Intelligent Storage Provisioning

```
[1] # vxassist -g diskgroupB make   volumeB1 100g mirror=faultzone
[2] # vxassist -g diskgroupB make   volumeB2 100g department=accounting
[3] # vxassist -g diskgroupB make   volumeB3 100g building=buildingA
[4] # vxassist -g diskgroupB mirror volumeB1
[5] # vxassist -g diskgroupB growby volumeB1 100g
```

Line `[1]` of Dialog 3-4 illustrates the intrinsic property of separation. The `mirror=faultzone` parameter indicates that the volume is to be mirrored, and that VxVM is to construct the mirrors on disks with different values for the `faultzone` attribute. Lines `[2]` and `[3]` illustrate the use of the user-defined parameters `department` and `building` to specify that volumes should be created from disks reserved for the accounting department or located in buildingA respectively.

The real value of Intelligent Storage Provisioning, however, is that it not only adheres to user intent when creating a volume, but it preserves that intent when extending it. For example, the command in line `[4]` of Dialog 3-4 adds a third mirror to `volumeB1`. Because `volumeB1` was created using mirrors in separate `faultzone`s, VxVM will ensure that the third mirror added when line `[4]` is executed is in a separate `faultzone` as well. Similarly, when the volume's size is increased by the command in line `[5]`, the intent that its mirrors be in separate `faultzone`s is preserved as well.

Combining the simplicity of the `vxassist` command with the generality of Intelligent Storage Provisioning simplifies virtual storage configuration while meeting and preserving enterprise intent for storage configurations in complex storage networks with advanced disk array capabilities.

Storage device portability

VxVM is unique among host-based storage virtualizers in that it supports all major UNIX platforms. This puts it in the unique position of being able to create virtual volumes that can be used by more than one platform. For example, volumes can be deported from a Solaris system and imported and used on an AIX, HP-UX, or Linux system. This feature of VxVM, known as portable data containers (PDC), lays the groundwork for serial data sharing—the use of data created on one UNIX platform by another UNIX platform of a different type. For example, files created on a Solaris platform can be transferred to a HP-UX or AIX platform for report generation or data analysis. Use of data on a platform different from the one on which it was created also requires that both platforms utilize common file system and file data formats. VxFS file systems use a common file system format across platforms, and a format that is convertible between UNIX and Linux. Some applications use platform-independent data formats; others, such as database management systems, provide filters for transporting data from one platform to another.

As more and more applications and data managers respond to the need to use the data they produce on different platforms, the ability to move volumes containing files and databases will be of increasing importance. VxVM provides the underpinnings for transferring data between platforms without the need for lengthy network copy operations or low-performing NFS cross-mounted file systems.

New in the Storage Foundation: multi-host coordinated storage management

Since its inception, VxVM has been a host-based storage virtualization manager. The locus of control and management of virtual volumes has been the host computer on which a VxVM instance is running. The scope over which a VxVM instance exercises control is the set of disk drives and LUNs that are accessible by the host on which it is running.

But the host-centric view is becoming less and less adequate as data center storage becomes more complex and the parts that comprise it become more interrelated. Recognizing the growing need of enterprises to manage their virtual storage across a broader front than the individual server, Symantec has begun the evolution of virtual storage management from host-centric to data center-wide with the introduction of the Storage Foundation Volume Server (SFVS).

To understand the volume server, it is helpful to review the functions that comprise host-based volume management. Figure 3-7 illustrates VxVM's position in the I/O stack, with emphasis on the two major functions it performs—control over virtual device configuration and in-line routing of application I/O requests.

Figure 3-7 Structure of host-centric VxVM storage virtualization

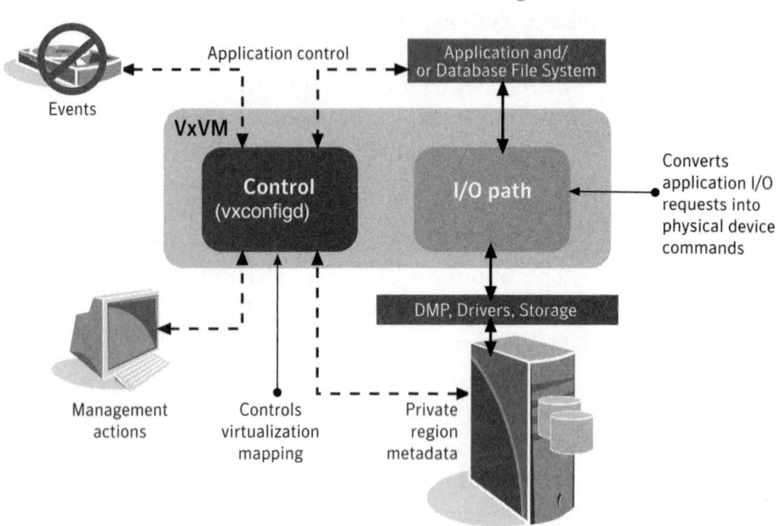

As Figure 3-7 suggests, VxVM has two primary functional components, an I/O path and a metadata management function. In the I/O path, VxVM transforms I/O requests to virtual devices made by applications (usually file systems) into read and write commands to the disks it controls, and issues the commands to operating system device drivers, or to DMP if it is installed.

The VxVM I/O path uses parameter-driven mapping algorithms to translate virtual I/O requests into physical commands. The parameters specify which block ranges of which disks represent which block ranges of which virtual devices. For example, for a mirrored striped volume, the principal parameters are:

- The disks containing the VxVM subdisks that make up the striped plexes, and their relative positions in the plexes
- Starting disk block numbers and sizes for each subdisk
- The stripe depth, or number of consecutive blocks that map to each striped disk

Striped, RAID5, and concatenated volumes are described by similar parameters.

These parameters are part of the VxVM metadata stored redundantly in disk groups' private regions. Managing them is the job of the other main component of VxVM—the metadata management function, known as the `vxconfigd` daemon. The `vxconfigd` daemon reads disks' private regions when VxVM starts up to retrieve the existing volume parameters that drive the I/O path. The control function also responds to external events that change the storage configuration, such as disk failure, commands issued by administrators, and API calls made by VxVM-aware applications like the VxFS file system. Whatever the source of an event, the `vxconfigd` daemon makes the appropriate changes to the parameters used by I/O path algorithms and records them persistently in disk private region metadata.

One of the great strengths of VxVM is that all configuration changes are transactional—a system may crash at any point during a configuration change, and upon restart, VxVM will either complete the transaction or reverse any operations it had performed prior to the crash.

The two-part structure of VxVM separates metadata management from the I/O path and makes it possible to optimize each to meet its primary requirement:

- Performance for the I/O path
- Transactional correctness for the metadata management function

This structure works well with individual hosts and homogeneous clusters whose complement of storage remains relatively static and separate from the rest of the data center. But with the number of servers and storage devices in a typical data center, and with increasingly frequent and dynamic reconfiguration of both, the host-centric structure has an inherent weakness, which Figure 3-8 illustrates.

Figure 3-8 The weakness of host-centric storage virtualization in a large data center

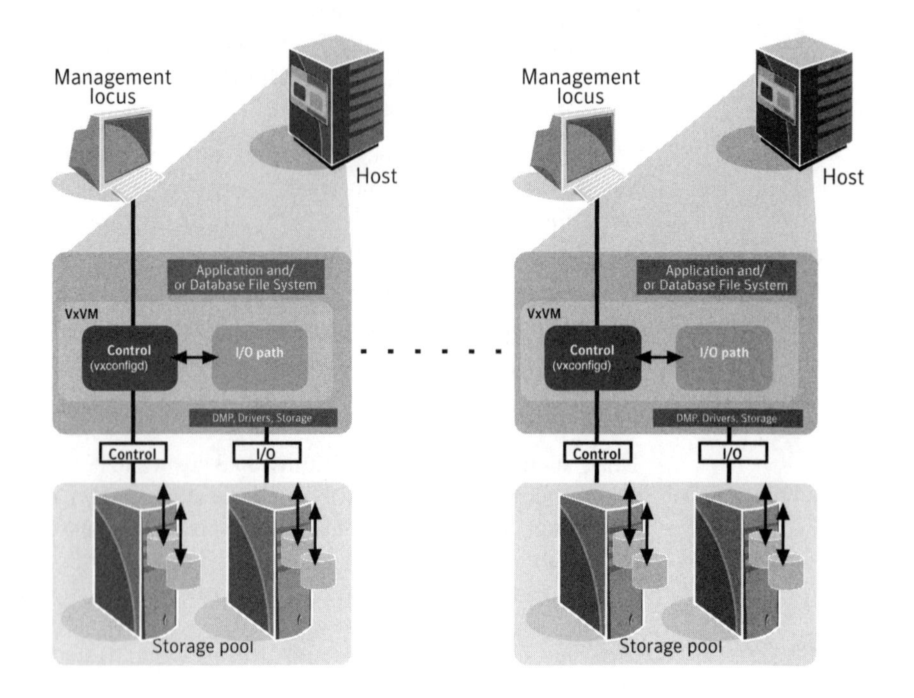

As Figure 3-8 suggests, each instance of VxVM in the data center represents a locus of control over storage virtualization for the host on which it runs. Effectively, this subdivides data center storage into separate pools, each dedicated to a single host or cluster. To be sure, CommandCentral and similar storage network management tools provide single management points for storage devices and network connections. Moreover, the architecture of VxVM itself makes it possible to move control of disk groups from host to host. What is missing, however, is a common view of entire pools of storage that may be shared among several hosts.

Consider, for example, the creation of a snapshot of volumes on Host A for use by Host B, perhaps to perform backup or data analysis while Host A is using the live data. To set up this relatively simple operation, the administrators for both hosts must collaborate:

- Host A's administrator creates the snapshot.
- When the snapshot is fully synchronized, Host A's administrator splits the disks that comprise it from their disk group into a new disk group, deports the

new disk group from Host A, and signals Host B's administrator that the group is ready.

- Host B's administrator imports the disk group (the two administrators must have agreed upon non-conflicting naming conventions for VxVM objects), and runs the applications that use the data on it.
- When the applications on Host B complete, Host B's administrator deports the disk group containing the snapshot and signals Host A's administrator that the group can be re-imported on Host A.
- Host A's administrator re-imports the snapshot group, rejoins it to its original group, and uses the VxVM FastResync feature to resynchronize its disks with the volumes from which they originated.

Given the value of the capability it enables (simultaneous processing of a frozen image of data by auxiliary applications while production applications continue to update live data), this process is not overly complex. In fact, it represents a common mode of operation for many data centers today. But useful as it is, the process has two inherent limitations:

- It relies on ad hoc cooperation and synchronization between two or more system administrators.
- It precludes off-host use of economical space-saving snapshots for such applications as low-impact incremental backup.

In this simple example, these limitations may not be severe—the two administrators may cooperate on a daily basis because they are part of the same application support team. But other common scenarios, for example, redeployment of storage capacity from one host to an unrelated one, are likely to involve administrators who do not collaborate closely in the normal course of business. Not only must administrators collaborate to achieve correct redeployments, but the systems for which they are responsible must have been configured with complementary (non-conflicting) storage naming schemes. Moreover, for ad hoc redeployment scenarios, there is no central location from which to discover excess storage capacity in the first place.

Both of the previously-mentioned limitations of host-based management of storage virtualization have a common root cause—the host-centric nature of the virtualization function. Each host has a view of the storage connected to and managed by it, but not of the entire pool from which it draws its storage. There is no systemic way for the administrator of Host B in the example above to know that a snapshot has been taken and is ready for use on Host B. There is no way for Host B to share access to the original volumes from which the snapshot was taken so that it could take advantage of low-impact space-saving snapshots for auxiliary applications.

The solution to these limitations, implemented in the Version 5 Storage Foundation Virtualization Manager, arises naturally from the two-part structure of VxVM shown in Figure 3-7. The performance critical component of VxVM is the I/O path, which must remain as short as possible. Direct communication from client host to storage device is a necessity. By comparison with application I/O, however, configuration-related operations are infrequent. Moreover, the first priority for configuration operations is transactional behavior rather than speed of execution. This suggests that the configuration control (metadata management) function of VxVM could be extracted from a group of hosts and centralized, and could exchange configuration state change information with VxVM I/O path functions running in each host over network links rather than via in-memory data structures.

Storage Foundation Volume Server does exactly this. It removes the volume configuration management function from a group of VxVM hosts to a central Volume Server which has visibility to all instances of VxVM running on hosts in the group as well as to the pool of storage they share. Figure 3-9 illustrates the structural change represented by the Storage Foundation Volume Server.

Figure 3-9 Storage virtualization with Storage Foundation Volume Server

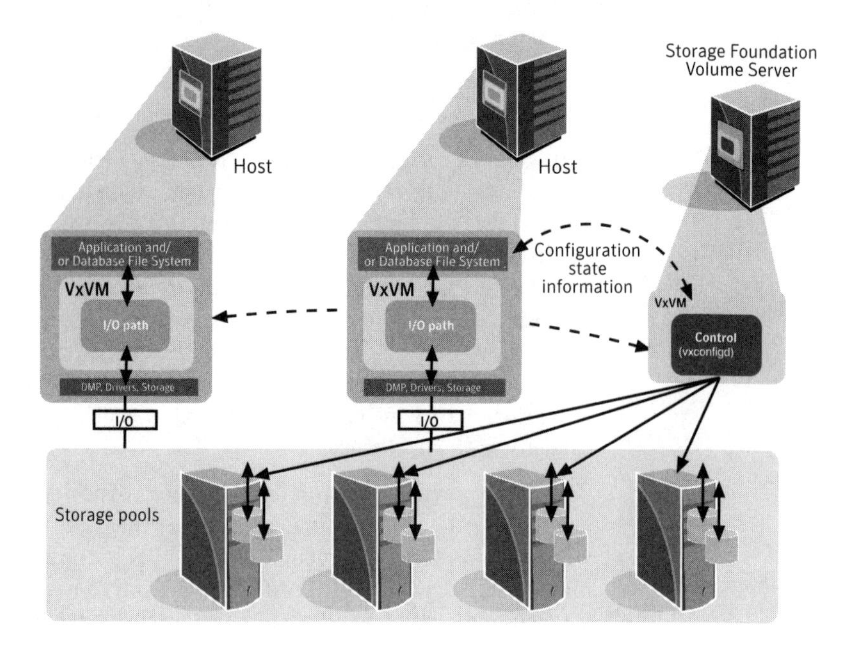

As Figure 3-9 illustrates, Storage Foundation Volume Server is a common metadata management function for storage virtualization that runs on a single server and provides configuration state information to a group of hosts (application or

database servers) running a variation of VxVM that is able to exchange configuration state information with the volume server. The volume server is failure-tolerant; a failover instance on an alternate host takes control of volume configuration and state management if the host running the primary instance fails. Hosts running the Volume Server variation of VxVM are referred to as virtualization clients.

A Volume Server instance is aware of the entire set of disk drives and LUNs that it is managing on behalf of all virtualization clients. It provides secure access to storage, making available only configuration information for volumes to which individual clients have access rights. Virtualization clients transform application I/O requests to virtual devices exactly as they do with host-centric VxVM (Figure 3-7), but report events such as disk failures and replacements that result in configuration changes to the Volume Server, which in turn, updates configuration information for all clients with connections to volumes that include the failed or repaired disk.

Using the Volume Server

The Storage Foundation Volume Server manages virtual storage using the same basic constructs that host-centric VxVM uses—disks, disk groups, subdisks, plexes, and volumes. The nature of these objects changes with multi-client visibility, however. In particular, a disk group, which is imported by a single server running host-centric VxVM, can be imported simultaneously by all virtualization clients in a Volume Server environment that are granted access rights to it. Simultaneous import of a disk group by multiple clients has the effect of creating a group-wide pool of storage that is accessible to all authorized application hosts as suggested by Figure 3-9, as opposed to the "pool per host" paradigm illustrated in Figure 3-8. With Volume Server, administrators can create multiple storage pools shared by a group of hosts, but this is typically done for business reasons rather than because of the host-centric nature of the virtualization technology.

To access a volume in a Volume Server environment, an authorized client uses a new VxVM operation, called "attach." (There is a counterpart "detach" operation.) Unlike the host-centric VxVM disk group split operation, the Volume Server attach operation does not change disk group membership, and as a result is a significantly faster way of transferring control of a volume from one host to another for off-host backup, data analysis, or other purposes.

Disk groups that are simultaneously accessible by multiple virtualization clients have another powerful advantage—off-host use of space-saving snapshots. As discussed earlier, space-saving snapshots can be created in seconds, and typically consume very little storage relative to full-copy ones. In principle, they are ideal for one-time off-host applications such as backup and analysis. Historically, however, this has not been possible because they retrieve images of unmodified blocks from original volumes, which must remain on host for production application use. For this reason, space-saving snapshots have been limited to on-host auxiliary applications, with potential adverse effects on the performance of production applications.

But with the Storage Foundation Volume Server, disk groups containing both original volumes and space-saving snapshots of them can be simultaneously accessible to multiple hosts, making it possible to use the space-saving snapshots for off-host auxiliary processing, as Figure 3-10 illustrates.

Figure 3-10 Off-host use of space-saving snapshots with Volume Server

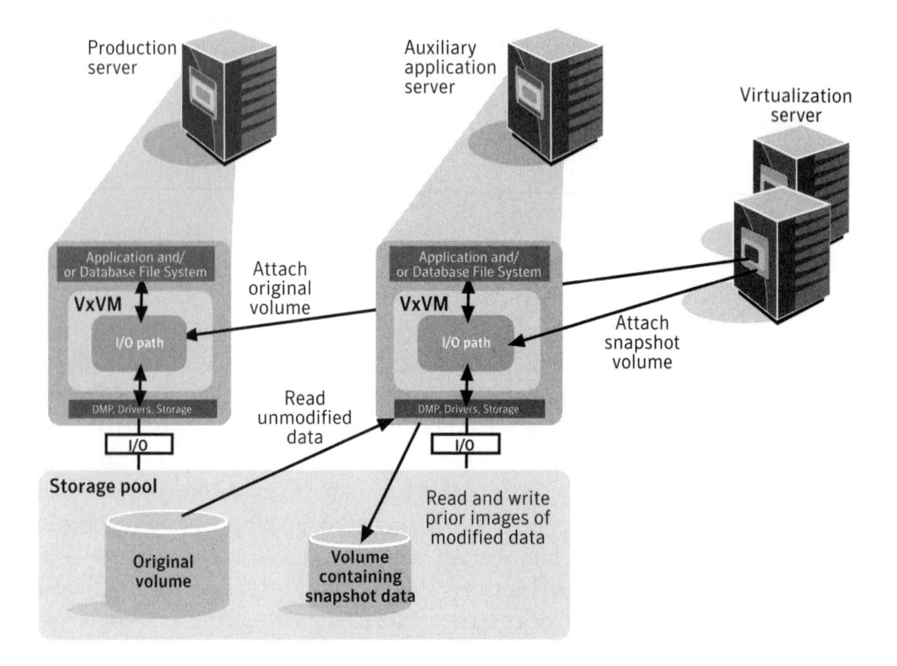

In Figure 3-10, the production server attaches the original volume, and production applications read and write data on it. At an application quiet point, the production server administrator takes a snapshot. Volume Server manages the data structures that comprise the snapshot, and can make them available to other virtualization clients that have imported the disk group containing them. It is thus possible for an auxiliary application server to attach a space-saving snapshot volume (all VxVM snapshots are presented to hosts as virtual volumes) and mount and access the file system on it.

When the auxiliary application server reads snapshot volume blocks that correspond to unmodified blocks of the original volume, its VxVM I/O path fetches the blocks' contents from the disks that comprise the original volume. When it reads snapshot volume blocks corresponding to modified original volume blocks, the VxVM I/O path retrieves the blocks' prior contents from the VxVM cache volume on which they were saved when the original volume blocks were modified for the first time after snapshot creation.

VxVM snapshot volumes can be written as well as read. With space-saving snapshots, on the first application write to a snapshot block range, VxVM allocates space on the snapshot volume, copies the contents of the corresponding block range from the original volume to it, and then overwrites the affected blocks in it. Because the disk group that contains both the original volume and the volume containing snapshot data is accessible to auxiliary application servers, they can update as well as read space-saving snapshots. Thus, with Volume Server, the range of potential off-host auxiliary applications is expanded to those that modify frozen images of production data as well as those such as backup that only read it.

Migrating to Volume Server

The Storage Foundation Volume Server introduced with Version 5 of the Storage Foundation represents a significant departure from earlier host-based virtualization techniques. The benefits of multi-host storage virtualization are clear from the preceding discussion; but for a complex data center to evolve from host-centric storage virtualization to the Volume Server approach requires significant planning and preparation. Symantec recognizes that many large enterprises use the Storage Foundation to manage their most critical data, and expects, therefore, that users will take the time to understand Volume Server constructs and capabilities thoroughly, evaluate carefully how those capabilities can best be used in their operations, and plan the transition conservatively for maximum benefit with minimum disruption.

Chapter 4

A closer look at the Storage Foundation core: the VxFS File System

This chapter includes the following topics:

- The role of file systems
- VxFS architecture
- Advanced VxFS features
- Summarizing the Storage Foundation basic components

The role of file systems

File systems are software programs that organize the undifferentiated numbered blocks presented by physical or virtual storage devices into files that are convenient for applications and human users to deal with. Compared to block-access storage devices, files are named more conveniently, and can be created, extended, truncated, deleted, and otherwise manipulated more easily. Applications and human users alike are very familiar and comfortable with the file paradigm. The software standardization organization for UNIX operating systems, POSIX, has created a standard for a file access application program interface set. The file access logic of applications that adhere to this standard need not be modified when the applications are translated, or ported, between different UNIX platforms.

Every commercial UNIX platform includes a POSIX-compliant native file system; some, like Linux, include several, allowing users to choose among them according to the file system attributes they value most highly. UNIX systems can operate with two or more file systems concurrently; each manages the block spaces of separate storage devices. When the Storage Foundation VxFS file system is installed, it either augments or replaces the native file system of the system on which it is running.

Since all commercial UNIX file systems are POSIX-compliant, all provide the same basic facilities to applications. File systems are therefore differentiated by other attributes:

- Robustness, or ability to survive and recover from system crashes, hardware failures, and application or user errors.
- Scaling, or ability to manage millions of files and terabytes of storage at practical performance levels.
- Advanced features, such as cross-platform portability, snapshots, and ability to support two or more cost-differentiated tiers of storage devices.

Robustness, scaling, and advanced features are the properties that differentiate VxFS from native UNIX file systems that are supplied with operating system platforms.

File systems' management of storage

A file system organizes the numbered blocks presented by one or more storage devices or virtual volumes into user files and metadata. A file system's metadata serves several purposes:

- It describes the block locations of the data in user files and certain common properties of the files, such as name, ownership, and access rights.
- It describes the tree-structured hierarchy in which files are logically organized.
- It describes the state of the storage device blocks managed by the file system, including which blocks are available for allocating new files and which ones are occupied by user data or other file system metadata.
- It describes certain properties of the file system as a whole, such as tuning parameters and characteristics of the volumes managed by the file system.

A critical aspect of a file system's design is the structure of its metadata and the algorithms used to manipulate it so that that the contents of the block space are always internally consistent, for example, so that every storage block is either marked available for use or is being used for exactly one purpose.

Because systems can crash while metadata updates are in progress, leaving the metadata in an inconsistent state, file systems that restart after stopping unexpectedly must ensure that their metadata are consistent before permitting users and applications to access files. File system checking, performed by a UNIX utility called `fsck` (file system checker) examines all file system metadata from multiple perspectives, for example verifying that no storage device blocks are lost (neither available nor allocated for some purpose) or allocated for more than one purpose (for example, to two files).

Metadata integrity verification after a system crash is a significant problem in file system design. The primary purpose of metadata checking is to ensure that a file system's metadata is consistent, so it must be exhaustive. But as files are added to a file system, the amount of metadata and its structural complexity both grow, and post-crash file system checking takes longer and longer. File system checking time is significant because applications cannot restart and users cannot access data after a system crash until file system structural integrity has been verified. A file system containing millions of files can take hours to check; these hours are additive to application downtime each time a system crashes, no matter how quickly the system is restarted. For this reason, enterprise file systems, including VxFS, log metadata operations that are in progress, and recover after system crashes by replaying the log to identify and repair metadata that might have been at risk.

VxFS architecture

One factor that sets VxFS apart from native UNIX file systems is that it was designed from the outset to scale to very large numbers of files and very large amounts of storage. Several design features contribute to the VxFS file system's ability to manage terabytes of storage and millions of files:

- Extent-based storage allocation describes large files very concisely, making the metadata structures that describe file data locations extremely compact compared to other UNIX file systems. Compact metadata results in less processing overhead, lower file system memory consumption, and faster reading and writing.
- Virtually all VxFS metadata is structured as internal files, making searching, integrity checking, and other metadata operations identical to user data access.
- Dynamic allocation of the inode data structures that describe individual files. Conventional UNIX file systems provide for a fixed number of inodes that is usually related to the capacity of the storage device managed by the file system, and therefore have a maximum number of files they can accommodate. In VxFS, the list of inodes that represent files is itself a file; when more files are added to the file system, the list can grow as a file would grow. There is no inherent limit to the number of files that a VxFS file system can accommodate.
- VxFS is a transactional file system, meaning that it operates on its metadata atomically—if a system hosting a VxFS file system crashes during metadata

operations, metadata operations can always be completed or backed out in their entirety when the system restarts so that the file system's structure remains consistent.

- VxFS is a logging, or journaling, file system, meaning that it keeps track of pending operations that might affect metadata integrity in a persistent intent log. When a system hosting a VxFS file system restarts after a crash, VxFS reads the file system's intent log and makes any necessary metadata repairs to restore file system structural consistency.

In addition to extreme scaling, the VxFS internal architecture enables important advanced features that differentiate it from typical native UNIX file systems:

- A common file system metadata format across all enterprise UNIX platforms means that VxFS file systems created on Solaris systems, for example, can be moved to and accessed directly by AIX or HP-UX systems. In conjunction with VxVM's Portable Data Container (PDC) technology, this means that a set of virtual volumes that contains a VxFS file system can be deported from one UNIX platform, and imported, mounted, and accessed directly by a different type of platform, without network copying or NFS cross-mounting.
- For transporting data between enterprise UNIX and Linux systems, a VxFS utility converts metadata to accommodate the byte ordering of the target system. This makes it possible to use data produced by so-called "big endian" systems on "little endian" systems, or vice versa, without network copying or cross-mounting.
- A single VxFS file system can span multiple virtual volumes with different I/O performance, availability and cost characteristics. This feature makes larger file systems possible, serving more users or applications, and resulting in fewer file systems to manage. Additionally, the VxFS Dynamic Storage Tiering facility, based on multi-volume file systems, implements user-defined policies for placing files on particular types of volumes and transparently relocating them to other volumes when conditions change. Dynamic Storage Tiering makes it possible for enterprises to implement multi-tier online storage strategies to realize cost savings without incurring offsetting administrative cost to ensure that files always reside the right type of storage devices to meet enterprise needs.
- A VxFS file system can take copy-on-write snapshots of itself almost instantly. These snapshots, called Storage Checkpoints, are persistent, and can be online for rapid recovery from user errors and other forms of data corruption whenever the file system itself is online. The metadata structure of VxFS makes file system performance nearly independent of the number of concurrently active snapshots.

The sections that follow describe these VxFS differentiators.

Extent-based Storage Allocation

In UNIX file systems, files are described by structures called inodes (information nodes). Every file and directory in a file system corresponds to a single inode. File systems maintain lists or other structures that aid in locating files' inodes so that the files themselves can be located and accessed.

An inode contains descriptive metadata about a file, its owner, an indicator of different users' rights to access the file, the times at which it was created, last accessed and last modified, its length, and so forth. Additionally, an inode contains a list of descriptors that identify, or map, the storage blocks occupied by the file's data.

While applications perceive a file as a single stream of consecutively numbered blocks, in fact, a single file's data may occupy many file system blocks scattered throughout the block space managed by the file system. When applications read or write file data, the file system uses the descriptors to map file blocks to file system blocks which it accesses to retrieve or store data.

In a conventional UNIX file system, space is managed in fixed-size file system blocks, typically 8 kilobytes in size. Since all blocks are the same size, a block can be completely described by its number. The data location descriptors in such a file system's inodes are therefore block numbers, or pointers to file system blocks. The first descriptor is the file system block number at which the first 8 kilobytes of the file are stored, the second descriptor is the block number for kilobytes 9-16 of file data, and so forth. For files that grow beyond their inodes' capacity for descriptors, usually about a dozen, the last few descriptors in the inode are conventionally used as indirect pointers—they contain the addresses of file system blocks that in turn contain additional block addresses (usually about 2,000 in each) where successive file data blocks can be found. Some file systems carry this one step further and reserve the last inode pointer as a double indirect pointer. It points to a file system block that contains pointers to 2,000 other file system blocks, each of which contains pointers to file system blocks that contain file data.

This mapping structure, illustrated in the diagram on the left of Figure 4-1, makes it possible for a UNIX file system to describe very large files, but it has three interrelated limitations:

- The size of the largest file that can be mapped by this structure, although large, is limited.
- Because a descriptor maps a relatively small amount of data (8 kilobytes), a large file requires a large number of descriptors. Even if consecutive data blocks are allocated, a descriptor is required for every file system block that contains file data.

- For all but the smallest files, locating file data blocks requires multi-level searching descriptor trees.

Figure 4-1 File structures in conventional and VxFS file systems

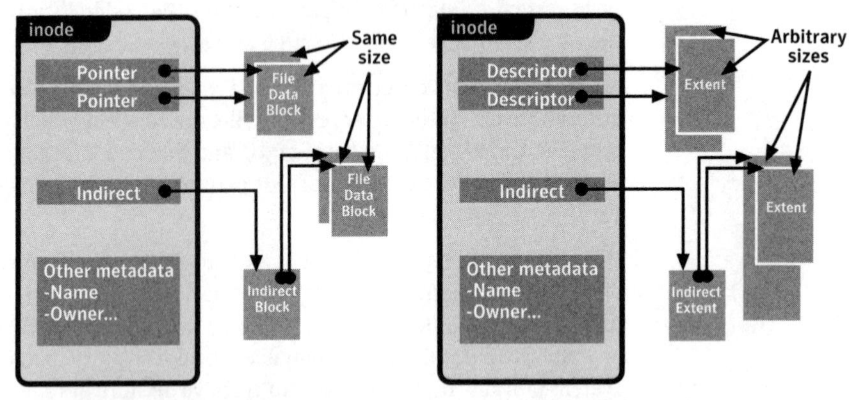

The VxFS file system has none of these limitations due to its use of a slightly different file data mapping structure shown on the right of Figure 4-1. A VxFS file system does have a file system block size, but rather than defining the unit in which storage is allocated, it defines the granularity with which storage is allocated. VxFS allocates storage to files in "extents" whose size may be any multiple of the file system block size. The file data descriptors in a VxFS inode differ from those in a conventional UNIX file system in that they contain both a starting block address and the extent size, or number of consecutive file system blocks mapped by the descriptor. Thus, if sufficient contiguous storage space is available on the device managed by the file system, and an application creates a gigabyte or larger file with a single request, the file can be mapped by a single extent.

Moreover, when an application extends the size of a file, VxFS allocates the additional space for extension from file system blocks contiguous to the file's last extent if possible. If contiguous allocation succeeds, there is no need to create an additional extent and consume an additional inode descriptor; the block count in the last existing descriptor is incremented to indicate that it also maps the newly-allocated extension space.

This space allocation scheme, known as extent-based allocation, makes it possible for VxFS to describe very large files very compactly. An inode can describe a multi-terabyte file without the use of indirect descriptors. VxFS does accommodate indirect extent descriptors for large files that are constructed by incremental extension, but these are only required when contiguous extension is not possible or when files are written randomly.

Extent-based storage allocation is particularly important for applications that process very large files. Because VxFS maps such files compactly (with a single descriptor where the file's storage is contiguous), converting file block addresses to file system block addresses when applications read and write data is simple and fast. Very large files can be created, because file size is not limited by a file system's ability to map a large number of file blocks. Extent-based storage allocation also minimizes the storage space consumed by metadata, making more of a file system's storage capacity available for user data. Moreover, it greatly reduces the amount of system memory required to hold metadata for open files. For example, in a conventional block-based file system caching all the metadata for an 8-terabyte file would consume 4 gigabytes of system memory, whereas with VxFS, a file of that size can be mapped by as little as a single extent descriptor.

Metadata structure and dynamic inode allocation

A file system necessarily imposes structure on the storage device blocks it manages so that it can locate files, manage free space, and store metadata related to the file system rather than to individual files. Different UNIX file systems structure the storage they manage in different ways, but all structures stem from a so-called superblock stored at some well-known storage device block address. A file system's superblock typically points to the locations of other structures, such as the inode list, the free space map, and so forth. It is the starting point from which all structures and data in the file system are found; if a file system's superblock is inaccessible, data in the file system cannot be located, even though it may be intact. In many file systems, the superblock is replicated so that the file system remains usable even if a hard error is experienced when reading the primary superblock copy.

Like other UNIX file systems, VxFS locates all data and metadata by referring to pointers in the superblock. VxFS is unique, however, in that virtually all of its metadata is structured as files, thus the algorithms used to manage metadata are the same ones used to manage user file data. For the most part, the fact that most VxFS metadata is structured as files is transparent to users. In one important respect, however, it is not.

VxFS inodes are stored in an inode list, which is itself structured as a file. As files are added to a file system, space for additional inodes can be allocated from the file system's free space pool whenever it is required. As files are deleted, their inodes are marked for reuse by other files. Because additional inodes can be allocated whenever they are needed, there is no inherent limit on the number of files that can be managed by a single VxFS file system. This contrasts with the conventional file system practice of reserving a fixed-size pool of inodes when the file system is created. For file systems of this type, administrators must estimate the maximum number of files that are expected to exist concurrently at any point in the file system's life. Once set, the size of an inode pool cannot be altered, so if all inodes are used, file allocations may fail even though there is space available on the device managed by the conventional file system. If a conventional file system typically contains a large number of files, administrators must monitor it so that inode overflow does cause file allocation failures resulting in application downtime.

Allocating space for inodes dynamically means greater flexibility and simplicity because there is no need to estimate how many files a file system will contain during its lifetime and size the inode pool accordingly. If a VxFS file system requires additional inodes, it allocates space for them from the file system's free space pool. As long as there is free space in the file system, files can be allocated.

Dynamic inode allocation has another important consequence for file systems that contain only a few files. Such file systems are commonly found in database applications, where the database management system uses a small number of files as containers for the data it manages. VxFS file systems used for this purpose allocate storage only for the inodes required to describe the required number of files. In large file systems, dynamic inode allocation can make gigabytes of additional storage available to applications compared to file systems that allocate inodes statically.

The internal architecture of VxFS has intangible benefits—the same compact, robust code paths that manipulate user data manipulate a file system's own metadata. But there are tangible benefits as well. Dynamic inode allocation automatically tunes the amount of storage space dedicated to file system metadata structures to match the number of files in a file system, conserving space for user files in file systems containing only a few files, and allocating additional inodes as required in file systems that manage large numbers of files.

Transactions and logging

If a file system is to preserve the integrity of the data it manages across system crashes, it must manipulate its metadata as transactions. The "ACID" properties of computer system transactions are discussed in VxVM transactions . In essence, each transaction must be independent of all others, must persist (for example, across system failures), and must either run to completion or disappear leaving no effect on the system.

Transactional properties are particularly important for file system metadata. For example, to extend a file's size, the file system must locate available space for the extension and remove it from the free space pool and update the file's inode structure to indicate that the newly-allocated space is part of the file. These operations require updates to separate metadata structures stored in blocks of the storage device managed by the file system. For performance reasons, the two updates typically overlap, as do similar updates made on behalf of other applications and users.

File system integrity can suffer if a system crashes during the execution of these updates:

- If the update that removes storage from the free space pool completes, but the update of file metadata does not, the space may be lost—not part of the free space pool, but not allocated to any file or other file system structure. Lost space may be a minor or major problem, depending upon the frequency of system crashes and the amount of space lost in this way.
- If file metadata is updated to indicate the extension, but removal of space from the free pool does not complete, a later file allocation or extension may use the same space again, resulting in the same file system blocks being allocated to two or more files. This is by far the more severe problem, because it is highly likely to result in corruption of user data.
- If neither update completes, the state in which the file system is left depends upon the atomicity of the two update operations. If an incomplete update leaves no trace, then file system integrity is not affected. If, however, an update could be partially complete, different types of file system corruption may result.

None of these situations are viable for a robust file system, so all file systems incorporate some form of transactional metadata updating.

Because system crashes can occur at any time, providing transactional semantics for file system metadata updates is a two-part problem:

- Updates must be sequenced so that the "window" of time during which the on-disk representation of metadata is inconsistent is both minimal and detectable.
- Upon restart after a system crash, a file system must ensure that its metadata is in a consistent state.

UNIX file systems solve the second part of this problem with a utility called `fsck` (file system checker). The `fsck` utility runs upon system startup for any file system that was not shut down properly (as for example, would happen in a system crash). It verifies the consistency of file system metadata, most importantly by making sure that there are no lost or multiply-allocated blocks in the file system's block space.

Simplistically, file system checking requires that the file data descriptors in every file's inode be cross-checked against others to detect multiple allocations, and against the file system's free space map to detect lost blocks. For file systems that contain large numbers of files, file system checking can take hours. This is problematic, because applications cannot use a file system until checking is complete. Therefore, the time it takes `fsck` to run is additive to the overall time to recover from system crashes, even in cluster environments where "recovery" means restarting an applications and all of its resources on alternate hardware. Minimizing post-crash file system checking time becomes an important design consideration for file systems targeted at enterprise-scale applications managing millions of files.

VxFS solves the problem of file system consistency checking by implementing a disk-based log, called the intent log, in which it records its intent to perform transactions that update metadata prior to actually performing them. When operations complete successfully, VxFS deletes their intent records from the log.

When recovering after a system crash, VxFS consults each file system's intent log, and repairs all metadata that might have been affected by the crash. For example, a file extension transaction is repaired by ensuring that the extended file's inode structure correctly maps the added space, and that the free space has indeed been removed from the file system's free space pool.

The VxFS intent log concept has a powerful implication for system availability. After a system crash, the time required for a VxFS file system to validate its metadata is related to the number of transactions that might have been in progress at the time of the crash rather than the size of the file system. For file systems containing millions of files, this can result in dramatically shorter recovery times. For example, with a file system containing a million files, if each of a thousand users was independently updating a different file at the time of a system crash, only a tenth of one percent of file system metadata would require validation upon crash recovery. There is no need to validate the remaining 99.9% of file system metadata because it was not being used at the time of the crash.

VxFS includes a full `fsck` utility for use in exceptional circumstances, for example, a hardware failure that destroys the intent log itself. In most cases, however, intent log playback is all that is required.

Even the most stable systems crash unpredictably on occasion. The VxFS intent log architecture minimizes the portion of overall crash recovery time attributable to file system metadata validation.

Performance optimizations

A fundamental value of any file system is the data integrity it provides. File systems deliver data integrity by delivering behavior specified in the POSIX interface standard, no matter what happens elsewhere in the system, including complete crashes.

As discussed earlier, UNIX file systems maintain metadata consistency across system crashes, generally by using logs to identify and repair metadata whose integrity was at risk at the instant of the crash.

Typically, however, UNIX file systems guarantee consistency for file system metadata only. They move data written by applications into a volatile cache, which is flushed to non-volatile storage either periodically or when certain events such as file system unmount occur. Caching data written by applications improves I/O performance, but creates a risk that data in apparently completed write requests can be lost if a system crashes before it has been flushed to disk.

For applications such as database management systems that take responsibility for the integrity of data within their files, this behavior is appropriate. For other applications, it may not be. There is no universal right answer to the tradeoff between user data integrity and file I/O performance. For this reason, the VxFS file system provides several different options that balance the two in different ways. These options, whose I/O performance and data integrity properties are summarized in Table 4-1, make it possible for administrators to tune either an entire file system or individual files for the appropriate tradeoff between high I/O performance and integrity of user data in the event of a system crash.

Table 4-1 VxFS cache flushing options

Option	Description
Cache completely disabled	User data in application write requests is written to non-volatile storage, and file system metadata is updated before request completion is signaled. Consequence: All completed application requests and all file metadata are up-to-date on non-volatile media after every I/O request.
Metadata updates deferred	User data in application write requests is written to non-volatile storage and any file extensions are reflected in non-volatile file metadata before request completion is signaled, but non-critical file system metadata updates are deferred. Consequence: Non critical file system metadata (e.g., `atime`, `mtime`) may be out-of-date upon recovery from a crash.
Data written directly from application buffers	Instead of moving data in application write requests from application buffers to file system buffers, VxFS writes it directly from the application's buffers. Consequence: Application is responsible for not modifying I/O buffer contents until writes are complete.

Table 4-1 VxFS cache flushing options *(continued)*

Option	Description
Cache flushed when file is closed	When an application closes a file, VxFS flushes all cached user data and metadata to non-volatile storage. Consequence: User data and metadata in files successfully closed by applications are up-to-date after recovery from a crash. User data may not have been flushed from files that are open at the time of a crash.
Cache tuned for expected I/O pattern	Individual files can be tuned to use file system cache appropriately for sequential or random-access I/O. For example, sequentially accessed can be "read ahead," and read cache can be disabled completely for randomly accessed files. Consequence: file system cache is used more efficiently.

These, and similar tuning options give application and database designers the flexibility to choose the right balance between maximum I/O performance and guaranteed integrity of user data across system crashes for every application.

Advanced VxFS features

The preceding sections discuss the basics of VxFS architecture—how the unique design of VxFS enables file systems to scale to meet common large enterprise requirements without sacrificing performance or data integrity. The VxFS architecture also incorporates advanced features that enable IT organizations to improve the quality of service they deliver to their clients:

- A file system metadata format that is common across enterprise UNIX platforms and easily convertible between UNIX and Linux makes it possible to move data between unlike UNIX platforms by transferring control of the storage devices that contain it, obviating the need for a physical copy or network cross-mount of the file system.
- The ability to spread a single VxFS file system across multiple virtual storage devices with different cost, availability, and performance properties makes it possible to exploit two or more "tiers" of storage to reduce overall cost without offsetting increases in administrative effort.
- A copy-on-write file system snapshot facility called Storage Checkpoints makes rapid recovery or data lost to procedural or user errors possible.

The sections that follow describe these features.

Cross-platform transportability

For a variety of reasons, most enterprise data centers include two or more UNIX platforms. For example:

- Applications often dictate the choice of platform. An enterprise may install a particular platform because it supports a key application, even though the enterprise may have standardized on a different platform for its general computing requirements.
- When enterprises merge with or acquire other enterprises, their information technology operations may include different platforms that cannot be integrated immediately.
- The trend of many data centers to deploy large numbers of interchangeable single-application Linux servers leads to mixes of Linux and enterprise UNIX servers.

Inevitably, as enterprises integrate their applications to provide holistic views of their operations, they encounter situations in which data generated on one type of platform must be used by another. This is challenging in two respects:

- The applications that produce data must produce it in a form that can be consumed by other applications. A few applications write data in the same format for all platforms they support. Increasingly, quasi-standard platform-independent data formats like MP3 and PDF are coming into common use. XML is sometimes used to universalize data. Other applications include filters that convert data created on one platform for use on another.
- Even if data in a file created by an application on one type of platform can be read by a related application on another platform, one platform's file system cannot usually be mounted on another type of platform because their metadata formats differ.

Conventionally, there are two common techniques that allow data to be transferred between unlike platforms.

- Data can be copied across a network from the system that produces it to a system that consumes it. While this is a useful technique, it requires significant network bandwidth and time, making it impractical for most large data sets.
- Data can be stored in a file server rather than on disks managed by a file system on the application host. Because file server access protocols (notably Network File System, or NFS) are standard across UNIX platforms, any type of UNIX platform can access data presented by an NFS file server. Again, this is a useful technique, but it constrains both the producing and consuming application platforms by the performance and scaling capabilities of the file server.

With Version 4 of the Storage Foundation, VxFS introduced an alternate solution to the problem of serial data sharing between UNIX platforms of different types. By using identical file system metadata formats across all supported UNIX platforms, VxFS makes it possible to mount and use a file system created on an AIX system, for example, on a Solaris or HP-UX system. Coupled with VxVM Portable Data Containers that allow control of virtual volumes to be transferred between unlike platforms, VxFS file systems make it possible to deport devices containing volumes hosting a VxFS file system from one host, and import, mount, and access it on another host of a different platform type. This is particularly significant for large data sets, for which copy times would be intolerable, or for particularly active ones, for which file server performance may be inadequate to meet application requirements.

Coupled with another Storage Foundation facility, full-copy snapshots, Portable Data Containers and transportable file systems enable valuable options for off-host processing of production application data. Figure 4-2 illustrates one such option.

Figure 4-2 Using transportable file systems for off-host backup

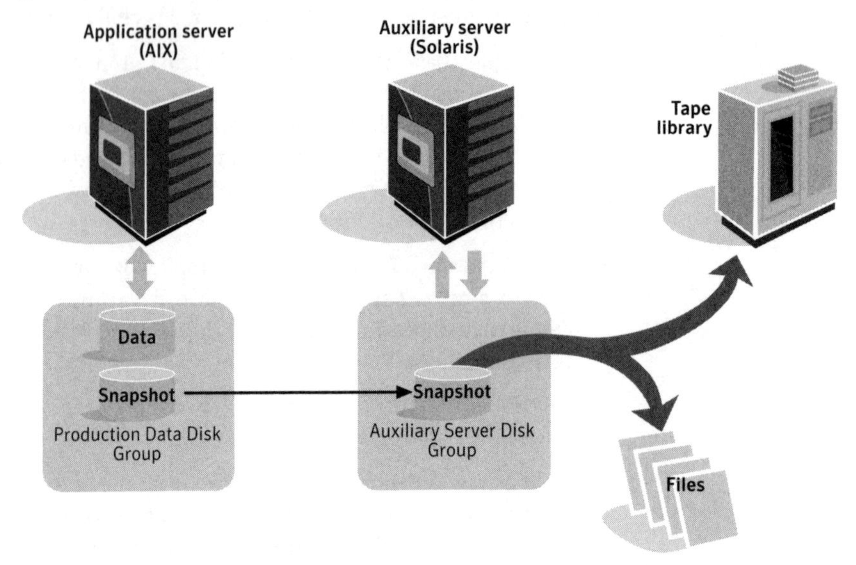

Figure 4-2 represents a production application running on an AIX server. At a time that is appropriate from an application standpoint (for example, close of business day), a VxVM Full-Sized Instant Snapshot of the production data is taken. VxVM synchronizes the snapshot volumes with the production data ones (makes the contents of the two identical by copying from the production volumes to the snapshot). When synchronization is complete, the disks containing the snapshot volumes are split from the VxVM disk group that contains them, deported from the production server, and imported on the auxiliary server.

Since they use the portable data container format, the VxVM volumes can be started on the auxiliary server. The VxFS file system(s) on them can be mounted and used directly, for example, for backup, report generation, data analysis, problem diagnosis, or software testing. Using the facilities of the Storage Foundation, the entire process can be accomplished while the production application is running. Because auxiliary processing uses different server and storage resources than the production application, it has no impact on production performance. The impact of resynchronizing snapshots with production data after they have been used is mitigated through the use of FastResync™ technology, and moreover, can be scheduled to occur at off-peak production times.

What is unique about this example is that the auxiliary server may be of a different type than the production server—Solaris and AIX in the figure. Thus, for example, if an enterprise has standardized on Solaris as its backup platform, Solaris can be used to back up AIX and HP-UX production servers' data. If data mining tools are only licensed for one of a data center's platforms, that platform can be used to analyze all platforms' data. As long as data within files can be interpreted correctly by both production and auxiliary applications, transferring data from one platform to another can be almost instantaneous, no matter what the size of the data set.

For auxiliary applications that run periodically, such as daily backups or weekly reporting, VxVM FastResync™ technology can be employed for rapid snapshot turnaround. When auxiliary processing of a file system snapshot is complete, the disks containing it can be deported from the auxiliary system, rejoined to their original disk groups, resynchronized with the volumes from which they originated, and transported to the auxiliary host again. FastResync™ technology resynchronizes volumes by copying only those blocks that change during the life of the snapshot, so it typically takes much less time than copying all blocks of the original volume.

Transferring data between UNIX and Linux systems running the Storage Foundation is similar, with one additional complication—conversion of metadata to accommodate the different ways in which different processor architectures address binary integers. The three major enterprise UNIX platforms all use the so-called "big-endian" format for interpreting two, four, and eight-byte binary integers. This means that of the bytes comprising an integer, the one with the lowest memory address contains the most significant eight bits, the one with the next-to-lowest memory address contains the second most significant eight bits, and so forth.

By far the most prevalent processor architectures on which the Linux operating system runs are those of Intel and AMD, both of which use the "little-endian" format for storing binary integers in memory. As the name implies, little-endian processors store the least significant eight bits of multi-byte binary integers at the lowest memory address, the next-to-least significant eight bits at the next-to-lowest memory address, and so forth.

File system metadata contains a large concentration of binary integers. Those occurring most frequently are the descriptors within inodes that contain block addresses of file data (and, in the case of VxFS, extent sizes). In order for a file system created on a big-endian (enterprise UNIX) system to be used on a little-endian (Linux) one, all integers in the file system's metadata must be converted from big-endian to little endian format. Integers can be converted all at once, before moving a file system from one platform to the other, or each time an integer in the file system's metadata is accessed. VxFS utilizes the former technique, accepting the one-time overhead of conversion in preference to the overhead of converting integer formats every time VxFS accesses file system metadata while the file system is in use.

To mount and access a VxFS file system from an enterprise UNIX platform on a Linux platform, the file system is unmounted, and a utility is run against it to convert its metadata to little-endian format. The disks containing the file system's volumes are then deported from the UNIX platform and imported on the Linux one, where the file system is mounted and accessed by auxiliary applications. With this additional step, even large enterprise UNIX file systems can be logically transported to Linux platforms, for example to perform off-host auxiliary processing of production data snapshots while the actual production data remains in use. As with UNIX-to-UNIX file system transportation, applications on both production and auxiliary systems must be capable of interpreting data within files correctly.

The ability to process data created and managed by one UNIX platform on a different UNIX platform or Linux increases the flexibility of enterprise information technology by making it possible to apply more types of resources to any given task. With the ability to transport file systems between unlike platforms, any available platform with appropriate software can be used for auxiliary processing without the need to copy data sets to it, or to restrict application performance and scaling to the capabilities of file server approaches.

Not only do transportable file systems have the potential to increase resource utilization, they also reduce the barriers to platform change by making it possible to use data from one platform on another immediately, without copy or conversion steps.

Multi-tier storage

Multi-tier storage—the deployment of virtual or physical storage devices with different I/O performance, data availability, and relative cost characteristics—is widely perceived as a means of reducing the average cost of data center online storage. The introduction of Serial ATA (SATA)-based disk arrays has increased user interest in multi-tier storage, but in fact, multi-tier storage has been available since the introduction of disk arrays and volume managers. The cost per usable gigabyte of storage differs, even when the same underlying device technology is used to implement it. For example:

- A mirrored LUN presented by a disk array or a volume mirrored by VxVM costs more per usable gigabyte than a RAID-5 or non-redundant one.
- Storage based on older, lower-capacity disk drives typically costs more per byte than storage based on newer, higher-capacity devices of the same performance class.
- LUNs presented by enterprise-class disk arrays typically cost more per usable byte than functionally-equivalent volumes constructed from directly connected disks of equivalent capacity and performance.

Information technologists are attracted to multi-tier storage primarily by the promise of cost efficiency. They reason that data objects that have different values to the enterprise should be stored on devices whose cost is commensurate with their values. Lower cost storage carries a penalty in terms of lower I/O performance or data reliability, but the reasoning is that lesser value of data justifies the lower service quality.

In many cases, the penalty is no penalty at all. In a typical data center, a large amount of the online data is accessed infrequently; it is online for policy or convenience reasons rather than frequent access. Such data is highly likely to be backed up as well. For data that is not accessed frequently, storage I/O performance is of little relevance. The ability to restore lost objects from a backup also leads to questions of the value of failure-tolerant mirrored configurations for such data.

In addition to cost, many enterprises create multi-tier storage hierarchies for non-technical reasons. For example, databases of business transactions or human resources records may be segregated from files containing engineering drawings for security reasons. The organization that owns a set of data, the applications that process it, and the I/O patterns to which it is typically subjected are also sometimes used as criteria for creating different storage tiers on which different types of data are placed. Controlling the placement of data objects within two or more tiers of storage can be useful to enterprises for several reasons:

- Different types of data have different I/O performance needs. Streams need high data transfer performance, but moderate I/O request rates are acceptable. Transactions need high I/O request rates but moderate data transfer performance.
- Applications that run concurrently may compete for I/O resources unless their data is placed on separate storage devices with separate access paths.

- Different data sets have different availability requirements. A typical enterprise can conduct business without its human resources system, but not without its point-of-sale or customer relationship management systems.
- Different data sets have different values. Loss of a day's business transactions is significant to an enterprise, but survivable. Losing annual closing figures might be catastrophic. Losing an entire day's work is significant to a video editor, but losing the finished product would be a much more serious setback for the organization.
- Enterprise accounting, security, and regulatory compliance policies may require that specific files or types of files be stored only on certain storage devices.

Getting value from multi-tier storage

Enterprises organize their digital information in files that are usually closely associated with business purpose—documents, transactions, images, audio tracks, and other digital business objects—each with a business value. Files are therefore obvious objects around which to optimize storage and I/O cost and performance.

The key to deriving value from multiple tiers of storage is to place each file on the appropriate type of storage device. More critical files should typically be placed on higher-performing, more reliable (and therefore more expensive) devices; less critical files can be placed on less costly ones that may deliver lesser service quality.

Matching a file to the right type of storage device is not difficult. Administrators can assign users or applications to different file systems on different devices. The challenge lies in the numbers, however. Placing millions of files on appropriate storage devices is far too time-consuming to be practical without either rigid structure or some form of automation.

Even more challenging is the fact that the right type of storage for a file varies with time. As a file ages, becomes inactive, grows or shrinks, or moves between directories, the right type of storage device for it changes. Manually relocating millions of files among tiers of storage devices would be a never-ending task. Automation is a necessity for utilizing multiple tiers of storage effectively, particularly for file systems containing large numbers of files.

Multi-volume file systems and the Dynamic Storage Tiering facility

The VxFS Dynamic Storage Tiering (DST) facility makes it possible to reap the cost and other benefits of multi-tier storage without incurring offsetting administrative cost. DST has two parts: multi-volume file systems and automatic policy-based placement of files within a file system's storage.

Multi-volume file systems, as the name implies, are file systems that occupy two or more virtual storage volumes. A VxFS multi-volume file system presents a single name space, so the existence of multiple volumes is transparent to users and applications. Internally, however, VxFS remains aware of each volume's identity, making it possible for administrators define policies to control the locations of individual files.

The VxVM volumes on which a multi-volume VxFS file system is constructed are known as its volume set. Volumes may be of different types (for example, striped, RAID-5, mirrored, and so forth) and may be based on different hardware technologies such as disk array LUNs of different types and directly attached disks of different technologies. Basing storage tiers on VxVM volumes provides an important advantage: volumes can be of any required capacity and configuration, even spanning multiple disk arrays if required for I/O performance or failure tolerance reasons.

Storage tiers and placement classes

Administrators of multi-volume VxFS file systems control file locations by defining file placement policies that specify both initial file location and the circumstances under which existing files should be relocated. A VxFS file placement policy consists of rules that restrict file locations to subsets of a file system's volume set. These subsets are called placement classes, and are typically identified with storage tiers. Files are created and extended within specified placement classes, and relocated to other placement classes when they meet certain qualifications.

For example, Figure 4-3 represents a volume set consisting of three placement classes called `tier1`, `tier2`, and `tier3`. This volume set might be suitable for a file system containing a few critical files (`tier1`), a larger number of files of average importance (`tier2`), and a still larger number of inactive files (`tier3`).

Figure 4-3 Example volume set for a multi-volume file system

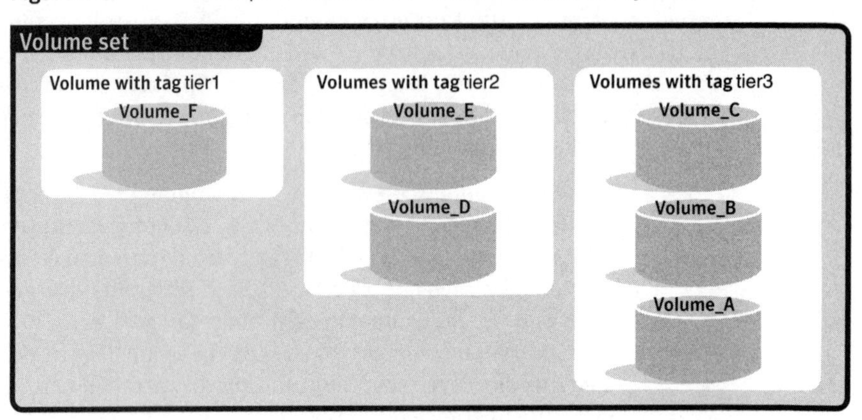

VxVM volumes are associated with placement classes by means of character strings called volume tags. In Figure 4-3, `Volume_F` carries the tag `tier1`, `Volume_D` and `Volume_E` are tagged `tier2`, and `Volume_A`, `Volume_B`, and `Volume_C` are tagged `tier3`. When placing files, VxFS treats all volumes in a placement class as equivalent, and balances space allocation across them.

A volume tag is simply a character string used to classify a volume. Any volume may be tagged with any convenient name. For example, it is common to name storage tiers after precious metals—`gold` (topmost tier), `silver` (middle tier), and `bronze` (lowest tier).

VxFS imposes no constraints on placement classes. Any volume may be added to any placement class by tagging it. It is good practice, however, to place volumes with identical, or at least very similar, performance and availability characteristics in a single placement class; in other words, to use the placement class concept to identify storage tiers.

File placement policies

VxFS allocates space for files in accordance with a file system's active file placement policy. A file placement policy consists of rules that govern the initial location and subsequent relocation of designated sets of files. A rule may designate the files to which it applies by name, by directory, by ownership, or by combinations of the three.

File placement policy rules specify file locations by placement class rather than by specific volume. This obviates the need to change the placement policy when volumes are added to or removed from a file system's volume set. Moreover, because placement class names need not be unique, one placement policy can be assigned to any number of file systems with similar requirements and storage complements.

File placement policy rules specify locations for both initial allocation and relocation as priority-ordered lists of placement classes. Files are allocated in the first class in the list if free space permits, in the second class if no free space is available in the first, and so forth. File allocation does not fail unless no space is available in any of the specified classes. This feature provides a "soft landing" for file systems in which a particular storage tier fills unexpectedly.

VxFS enforces file placement policies on administrative command. Policy enforcement is typically scheduled at regular intervals (for example, daily), at times when production activity is expected to be low. During policy enforcement, VxFS relocates files to the first placement class listed in the rule that applies to them if space is available, to the second class if no space is available in the first, and so forth.

File placement policies may specify unconditional relocation; alternatively, relocation may be based on qualifications such as time since most recent access or modification, access intensity (sometimes called I/O temperature), and file size.

File placement policies are deliberately not file system-specific. In data centers with many similar systems, for example, web or database servers, a single file placement policy can be assigned to all file systems with similar requirements and storage configurations. As long as the volumes containing a file system are tagged appropriately, the same policy can be assigned to it. This promotes storage and data management consistency—similar files are subject to the same policies—without requiring constant administrative attention across a number of systems. Storage Foundation Management Server, discussed in Chapter 6, can be used to store file placement policies in a central database, and assign them to file systems throughout the data center.

Metadata and availability in multi-volume file systems

VxFS multi-volume file systems also provide a mechanism by which administrators can control the location of metadata within a file system's volume set. Individual volumes can be designated as eligible to contain metadata or restricted to holding only user data. The first volume in a volume set is always eligible to contain metadata.

A multi-volume file system can be mounted and accessed as long as all of its metadata is accessible. If volumes that contain only user data fail, the file system can still be mounted and data on the surviving volumes accessed. Administrators can make volume(s) that can contain metadata highly failure tolerant, and tune the availability of other volumes to the requirements of files that are placed on them according to policy.

Summarizing the Dynamic Storage Tiering facility

A two-tier online storage strategy, in which the second tier is used to store inactive or non-critical files, can reduce a data center's average cost of online storage by 30% or more. Multi-tier storage can also be used to segregate data by access characteristics or other business properties. The VxFS Dynamic Storage Tiering facility automates the placement of files across storage tiers, ensuring that files are allocated in the proper locations and moved to alternate locations when conditions change. With Dynamic Storage Tiering, storage hardware savings can be realized without becoming subsumed by increased administrative cost.

Storage Checkpoints

The VxFS file system includes a space-saving snapshot facility called Storage Checkpointing. Storage Checkpoints are persistent, writable, point-in-time snapshots of a file system. Storage capacity for Storage Checkpoints is allocated from within the space managed by the file system, so a file system and its Storage Checkpoints are completely self-contained. Storage Checkpoints are created by administrative command, and exist until deleted administratively, or until the space they occupy is required for other purposes. For applications that use multiple file systems, Storage Checkpoints of all file systems can be coordinated so that they occur at the same logical instant. Figure 4-4 illustrates the relationship of Storage Checkpoints to their parent file system.

Figure 4-4 Storage Foundation Storage Checkpoint

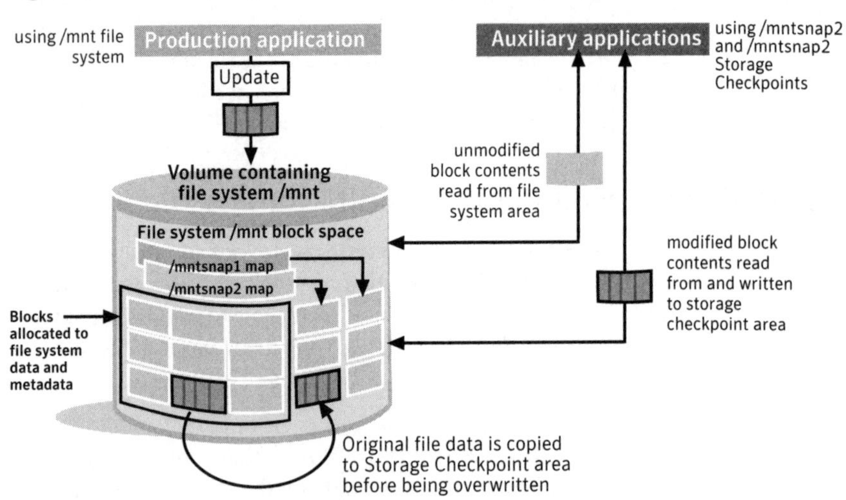

As Figure 4-4 indicates, Storage Checkpoints are entirely contained within the file system block space, and require no external volumes or other structures. This makes them extremely simple to administer. Because they are entirely contained within a file system's volume set, additional space for either Storage Checkpoints or file data can be allocated in a single operation using the Storage Foundation integrated volume and file system expansion capability.

In essence, a Storage Checkpoint consists of a copy of the file system's inode list that is initially populated with so-called overlay descriptors that point to the data in each file. Because virtually every metadata structure in a VxFS file system is a file, an inode list describes both data and metadata.

As files are updated, VxFS replaces overlay descriptors in the Storage Checkpoint inode list with descriptors that point to images of the pre-update block contents. Storage Checkpoints are transparent to production applications that read and write data in the main file system (there is a small performance penalty for the first update to a block after the snapshot is created).

When application requests to the main file system result in data or metadata updating, VxFS first determines whether updated blocks have been modified since the most recent Storage Checkpoint was created. When a block is updated for the first time, VxFS copies its contents to space allocated from the file system's free pool and updates the Storage Checkpoint's map to point to the copy before writing the update in the original location. Thus, the first application update to a file system block after creation of a Storage Checkpoint typically takes longer than subsequent ones.

Storage Checkpoints can be mounted as if they were file systems and read and written by on-host auxiliary applications immediately upon creation. When an application reads data from a Storage Checkpoint, VxFS consults the checkpoint's map to determine whether requested blocks have been modified. If they have not, main file system blocks are read. If they have, VxFS uses the checkpoint map to locate prior contents of the modified blocks and reads or writes those to satisfy the application request.

The regular internal structure of a VxFS file system that makes it possible to describe an entire Storage Checkpoint with an alternate inode list also makes possible the advanced capabilities listed in Table 4-2 that further enhance the utility of Storage Checkpoints.

Table 4-2 Advanced capabilities of Storage Checkpoints

Advanced capability	Value proposition
Linked Storage Checkpoints	Each Storage Checkpoint is linked to the next (newer) and previous (older) ones for the same file system (if they exist). This structure makes file system write processing time independent of the number of active checkpoints, and at the same time makes it possible to delete a Storage Checkpoint without affecting older or newer ones.
Storage Checkpoints of Storage Checkpoints	To an auxiliary application, a Storage Checkpoint is a file system. Because they are writable, Storage Checkpoints can be used to test software, explore "what if" scenarios with new applications and data models, and so forth. A Storage Checkpoint of a file system can itself be checkpointed before being used for destructive testing. After testing, the original checkpoint can be restored from the secondary one for a second test with the same initial data, and the procedure can be repeated indefinitely.

A file system can be rolled back to any active Storage Checkpoint as a starting point for recovering from data corruption. To restore a file system from a Storage Checkpoint, VxFS replaces the main file system's inode list with that of the Storage Checkpoint, and deletes all active checkpoints that are older than the restored one, returning the storage they occupy to the free space pool. Restoration is fast, because little or no data is copied. Moreover, any checkpoints that are newer than the restored one are preserved.

Symantec NetBackup uses a special type of checkpoint, called a "no-data" Storage Checkpoint, to implement a block-level incremental backup facility for databases that use VxFS file systems as their underlying storage. Conventional incremental backup techniques are based on file activity–if a file is modified, however slightly, the entire file becomes part of an incremental backup. They are ineffective with databases that use file systems to contain their data files, of which there are typically a small number. Database management systems typically update all of their data files each time a database is started, making an incremental backup of database data essentially equivalent to a full backup.

No-data checkpoints map modified file system blocks, but not their prior contents. They are effectively lists of file system data and metadata blocks that have changed since a given point in time. Symantec NetBackup uses the information in a no-data Storage Checkpoint to create a block-level incremental backup of a file system that contains only the contents of file system blocks that have changed since checkpoint creation. A block-level incremental backup can be restored over an image of a file system that has been restored from an earlier full backup or normal Storage Checkpoint to bring it to a more recent recovery point.

Storage Checkpoints enable a variety of sophisticated storage and data management techniques. A checkpoint can be used to back up or analyze ("mine") a point-in-time image of a file system while the actual file system is in use. They can be used for tests of software updates and user data structure changes that require modification of the data being tested against. They can be kept online for a limited period, making it possible for users to recover erroneously deleted or corrupted files. Storage Checkpoint creation and deletion are scriptable operations, so short-lived Storage Checkpoints can easily be made part of periodic management procedures.

Summarizing the Storage Foundation basic components

The VxVM volume manager and VxFS file system provide enterprise-class basic storage management for enterprise UNIX and Linux systems. Their storage virtualization and file management capabilities are robust, scalable, and high-performing, but more importantly, advanced capabilities like snapshots and Dynamic Storage Tiering both simplify storage administration and improve quality of storage service in large, complex data centers.

Integration between VxVM and VxFS creates additional synergies that further streamline data center operations, for example, by automatically increasing the size of virtual volumes when a file system is expanded, or by automatically freezing file system activity and flushing caches when a volume snapshot is taken. Integration with adjacent applications, such as backup and database management systems, adds additional value. For example, using block-level incremental technology, backup administrators can take incremental backups of databases that are truly incremental. Storage Foundation-based database editions provide seamless restore and resynchronization of databases from low-impact snapshot-based backups.

Yet another powerful advantage of the Storage Foundation is the common administrative look and feel it presents across all enterprise UNIX and Linux platforms. Not only does the common look and feel reduce administrative training cost, but by increasing administrative familiarity with a single way of doing things, it tends to reduce human error in the data center.

With the common administrative paradigm they present, VxVM and VxFS together form the basis for data center-wide consolidated management of storage. The chapters that follow discuss how the Dynamic Multi-pathing facility helps keep data accessible in complex storage networks, and describe the Storage Foundation

Management Server that consolidates monitoring and active management of large numbers of servers running the Storage Foundation into a single location.

Chapter 5

A closer look at the Storage Foundation: Dynamic Multi-pathing

This chapter includes the following topics:

Robust access to networked storage devices

As data centers have increasingly adopted storage networks, the network itself has become an important factor in delivering data availability. Not only must virtual storage devices be robust, but access to the physical devices that comprise them must be proof against failures as well. The primary technique for making the host-to-storage device connection failure-tolerant is to provide two or more paths between the two. If one path fails, communications can continue using an alternate one.

Making storage network hardware robust

One way to make connections between hosts and storage devices robust is to install two completely separate storage networks, or fabrics, each with connections to both hosts and storage devices. Figure 5-1 illustrates such a configuration.

Figure 5-1 Multiple paths to networked storage devices

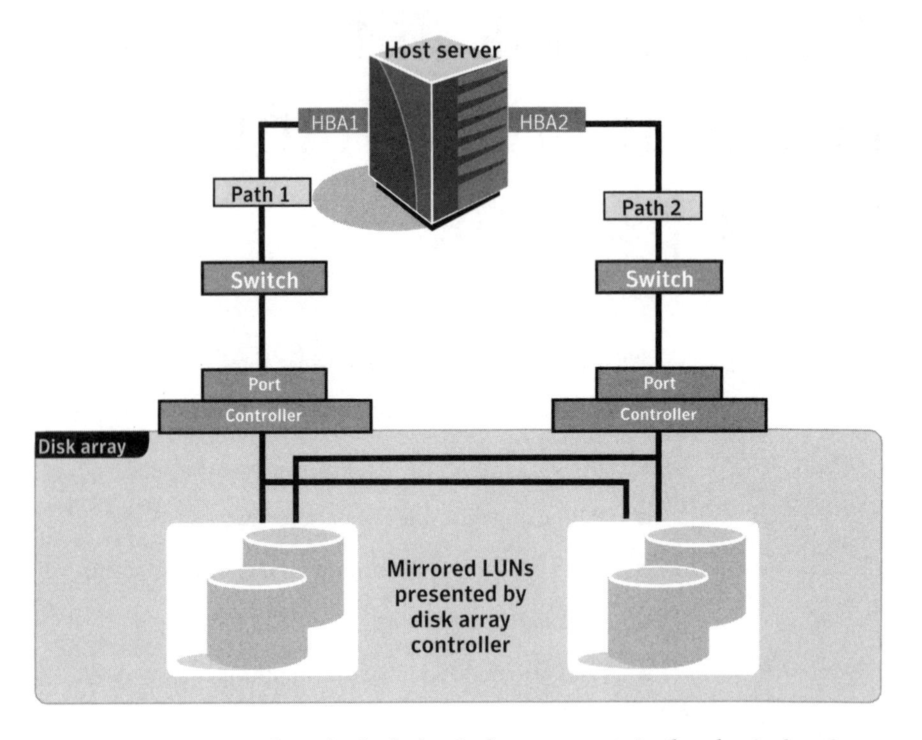

Figure 5-1 represents the principal physical components in the physical path between hosts and storage devices (in this example, mirrored devices virtualized and presented as LUNs by disk array firmware).

- Host bus adapters (HBAs) provide the interface between host memory and storage network protocols, and connect via cables to ports on storage network switches.
- Switches route messages between ports connected to HBAs and ports connected to disk array controllers.
- Disk array controllers provide the interface between disk array internal protocols and storage network protocols.

As Figure 5-1 suggests, providing two completely separate paths between hosts and storage devices allows continued communication between the two if a failure occurs anywhere in one of the paths. Variations of this configuration are often implemented. For example, some enterprise-class storage network switches (called directors) are designed to be internally failure-tolerant. In networks built using these devices, completely separate fabrics may not be necessary. However storage network failure-tolerance is achieved, the key point is that multiple paths to critical devices cannot share components that are not failure-tolerant.

The storage I/O stack

Figure 5-2 provides an overview of the principal functions performed in a UNIX storage I/O software stack, both with and without host-based virtualization and path management. While different platforms' implementations differ in detail, UNIX I/O software stacks share the common overall structure illustrated in Figure 5-2, simply because they all perform the same basic functions.

In systems with no host-based virtualization, file systems (and database managers that are configured to use so-called raw devices) make I/O requests directly to operating system drivers that interact with disk drives and LUNs via host bus adapters. Path [1] in Figure 5-2 represents a direct software interface between file system and storage device.

UNIX operating system drivers consist of:

- A SCSI layer that transforms operating system I/O requests into the form required by the storage device (e.g., SCSI Command Data Blocks, or CDBs)
- A host bus adapter (HBA) layer that interacts with HBAs to set up the transfer of commands, device responses, and data between host and storage device

In the scenario represented by path [1] in Figure 5-2, the file system makes I/O requests directly to the operating system's SCSI driver, which reformats them as SCSI commands and passes them to the HBA driver for transmission to the addressed device. HBA drivers transmit commands and receive responses without interpretation. For performance reasons, direct memory access (DMA) hardware is typically used for data transfer, but data transfer occurs on the path used to issue the command that causes it.

Figure 5-2 Variations of the UNIX I/O software stack

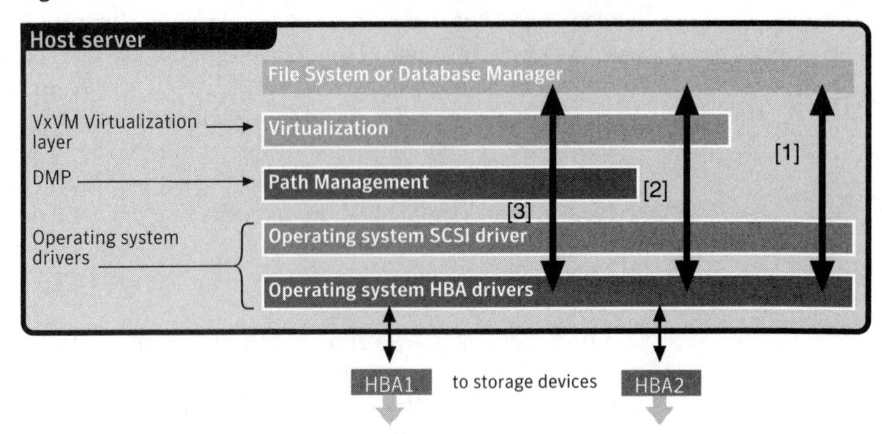

Host-based virtualization software

Host-based storage virtualizers like VxVM add a layer to the I/O software stack. The virtualization layer manages sets of storage devices which it represents to file systems and database managers as disk-like virtual volumes. Path [2] in Figure 5-2 represents the software stack traversed by file system I/O requests made to virtual volumes. In this scenario, the virtualization layer transforms file system I/O requests into storage device commands addressed to disk drives and LUNs, and issues them to operating system drivers.

For example, VxVM transforms each application write request to a mirrored volume into a write command to each of the volume's mirrors, and each read request into a read command to one of the mirrors. More complex transformations also occur. For example, a VxVM transforms a write request to a RAID volume into a series of read and write commands interspersed with parity computations, all of which collectively maintain parity consistency when user data is updated.

UNIX operating systems typically identify each unique storage network address (path) with a single storage device. If a device is accessible on two or more network addresses, it is treated as two or more unique devices. In order for a volume manager to use a multipath device, the device must be virtualized, and presented as though there were only one path to it. Virtualizing multipath disk drives and LUNs requires a layer of software between the volume manager and the operating system device driver to route each I/O command on one of the paths to the device it addresses.

Path [3] in Figure 5-2 represents the I/O stack with path manager present. In this scenario, commands issued by the virtualization layer are intercepted by the path manager, which determines which path to use to communicate with the addressed device, and issues the command to the operating system driver on that path.

Disk array support for multipath access

A complicating factor for multipath access to disk array LUNs is that different disk arrays support multipath access to LUNs in different ways. Fundamentally, there is a distinction between:

- Disk arrays that can execute commands to a single LUN on two or more array controllers simultaneously. Such arrays are called active-active. If a path to an active-active array fails, commands can be rerouted to other paths, maintaining continuous access to data.
  EMC's Symmetrix and DMX arrays, Hitachi Data Systems' 9900 Series (Lightning), and IBM's ESS series (Shark) are active-active arrays.
- Disk arrays that can only execute commands to a LUN on one controller, but can switch, or "fail over," LUN access to an alternate controller if necessary. Such arrays are called active-passive.
  EMC's Clariion Cx600 and Cx700, Hitachi Data Systems' 95xx and 9200 series, IBM FASt-T, and Sun's T3 and T4 are active-passive arrays.

In addition to this broad classification, active-passive disk array capabilities differ in three ways that can affect availability and I/O performance:

- Active-passive arrays that can simultaneously execute commands to a single LUN received on two or more ports of the same array controller are called active-passive concurrent arrays. Active-passive concurrent arrays' LUNs fail over to secondary controller paths only when all primary controller paths have failed. Most active-passive arrays can be configured for active-passive concurrent operation.
  EMC's CLARiiON, Hitachi Data Systems' 9500V series, IBM's FASt-T, and Sun's T3 and T4 are active-passive concurrent arrays.
- Some active-passive arrays fail over from primary to secondary paths automatically when they receive commands to a LUN on a secondary path. Others fail over only on receipt of explicit commands from their hosts. Explicit failover simplifies support for active-passive arrays in clusters, where multiple hosts can issue commands. Without explicit failover, cluster software must synchronize all hosts' access to a LUN before initiating implicit failover so that I/O requests from multiple hosts do not lead to continuous failovers.
  Sun Microsystems T3 and T4 arrays are capable of explicit failover.
- Some active-passive arrays can fail entire groups of LUNs over together rather than one-by-one. If all primary controller paths to a LUN in such an array fail, all LUNs in its group fail over to secondary paths. LUN group failover is faster

than individual LUN failover, and can therefore reduce the application impact of an array controller failure, particularly for disk arrays that present large numbers of LUNs.

Hitachi Data Systems' 9200 series arrays are capable of LUN group failover.

DMP: using multiple I/O paths effectively

Effective use of multiple I/O paths requires both awareness of storage network topology and an ability to respond rapidly and automatically to changing conditions in the storage network. The Storage Foundation Dynamic Multi-pathing (DMP) facility automates multipath management in accordance with pre-defined policies. DMP enhances system availability and I/O performance in three ways:

- DMP improves data availability. If an I/O path fails, DMP automatically reroutes commands addressed to it on alternate paths. Rerouting is transparent to storage applications. When a failed path returns to service, DMP restores the original configuration automatically and transparently.
- DMP improves I/O performance. For disk arrays that support simultaneous multipath access to a storage device, DMP distributes I/O commands across all available paths using one of several pre-defined multipath I/O load balancing policies.
- DMP improves application resiliency. In cluster configurations, DMP improves system availability by eliminating application failovers that might otherwise result from I/O path failures.

DMP is an integral feature of the Storage Foundation Volume Manager, VxVM. When DMP is enabled, administrators can manage both storage virtualization and I/O path policies from a single console or graphical interface.

DMP in the UNIX storage I/O software stack

DMP operates as a layer in the UNIX storage I/O software stack. Figure 5-3 shows a simplified model of a generic UNIX storage I/O software stack that includes the VxVM virtualization layer and the DMP path management layer.

Figure 5-3 VxVM and DMP in the UNIX I/O software stack

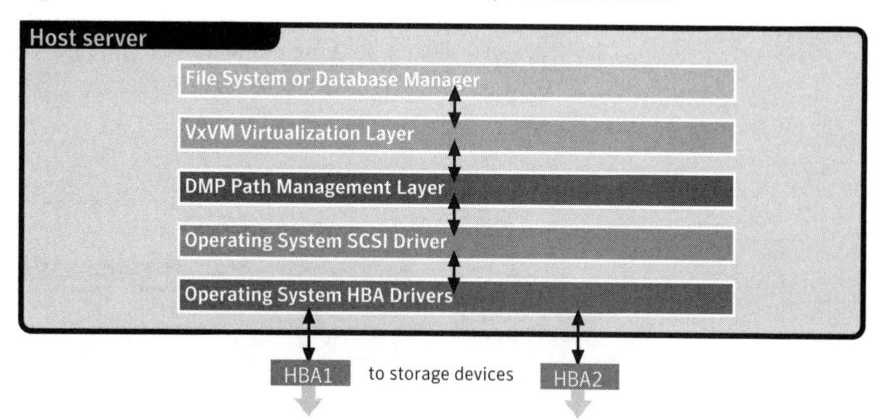

In a typical server, almost all I/O requests to virtual or physical storage devices are issued by a file system (in a few cases, database managers issue I/O requests directly to raw devices). The VxVM virtualization layer converts these requests into appropriate sequences of read and write commands to physical disks or LUNs. DMP is below the virtualization layer in the I/O stack in the sense that it receives I/O commands from the VxVM virtualization layer, chooses a path (essentially an HBA) for each one, and issues it to the operating SCSI system driver for execution.

DMP support for disk arrays

Supporting multiple access paths to disk array LUNs requires awareness of individual arrays' characteristics. DMP has a modular architecture that makes it possible to integrate support for different types of multipath access control quickly and easily.

Disk arrays with multipath LUN access capability may be supportable by DMP without custom software. DMP can manage multipath access to a disk array's LUNs by treating them as disks, provided that the array has the following properties:

- LUNs are active-active
- LUNs respond to SCSI inquiry commands with unique serial numbers, and each LUN's serial number is reported identically on all paths
- LUNs' unique serial numbers can be read from the SCSI standard mode page location

If an array has these properties, DMP can treat its LUNs as though they were disk drives; no special support is required. For arrays that require more specialized handling, the DMP architecture provides for array support libraries (ASLs) that discover and configure LUNs, and kernel-mode array policy modules (APMs) that perform array-specific functions in the I/O path. Figure 5-4 illustrates how ASLs and APMs fit into VxVM's configuration facilities and I/O path.

Figure 5-4 The DMP Device Discovery Layer (DDL) architecture

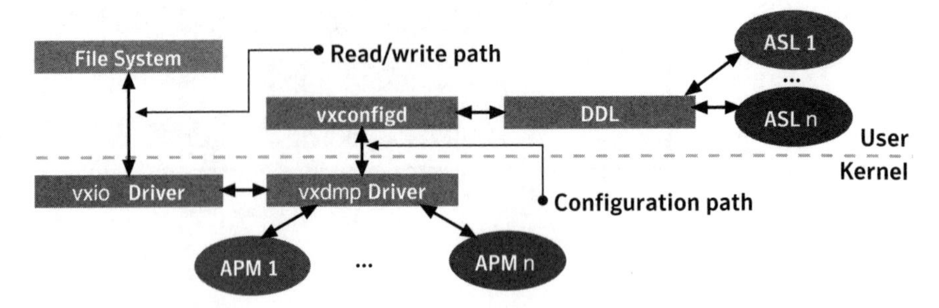

For each device it discovers, the VxVM Device Discovery Layer (DDL) calls each installed ASL in turn until one claims the device based on its vendor and product identifiers. The claim associates an array model with the device, which in turn determines the set of APMs that the VxVM I/O path invokes to perform such functions as path selection, path failover, and SCSI reservation and release.

DMP and device discovery

UNIX operating systems discover the storage devices that are accessible to them when they start up by probing their I/O buses and storage network connections. Following operating system discovery, the VxVM configuration daemon, `vxconfigd`, performs its own discovery phase to determine which devices discovered by the operating system are accessible on multiple paths.

For each disk or LUN it discovers, a UNIX operating system creates data structures called nodes in its device tree. For example, the Solaris operating system creates nodes in the `/dev/rdsk` and `/dev/dsk` branches for each disk drive or LUN it detects. For devices that are accessible on two or more paths, operating systems create separate nodes corresponding to each path, effectively treating each path as a separate device.

During its path discovery, the VxVM `vxconfigd` daemon identifies multipath devices by requesting unique product information from each operating system device. Ostensibly different operating system devices that respond with identical product information actually represent multiple paths to the same device. The daemon creates structures called metanodes in the Storage Foundation branches of the device tree for each unique storage device it detects.

VxVM metanodes represent virtualized metadevices. Each metadevice consists of a disk or LUN plus all I/O paths on which it can be accessed. Figure 5-5 shows the relationship of DMP metadevice nodes and operating system device tree nodes for single and dual-path devices in the Solaris environment.

Figure 5-5 VxVM Subtree for a single-path device (Solaris)

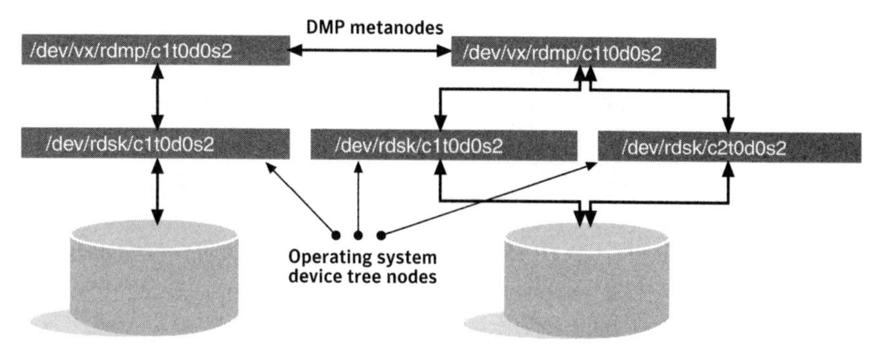

With DMP, the VxVM virtualization layer issues its I/O commands to metadevices rather than directly to operating system devices. DMP passes commands to single-path devices through to the operating system driver. For multipath devices, DMP chooses a path on which to pass each command to the operating system according to the load balancing policy in effect for the metadevice.

DMP I/O load balancing policies

DMP's primary purpose is to keep data available by keeping storage devices accessible when I/O paths fail. When all paths are operating, however, DMP can also improve I/O performance by routing each command on the optimal path. Administrators can set one of six different policies to define how DMP routes I/O commands for a given device:

- Balanced path
- Round-robin
- Minimum queue length
- Adaptive
- Priority
- Single active path

The sections that follow describe these six policies.

Balanced path routing

DMP's balanced path policy divides a device's block address space into as many disjoint regions as there are active paths, and routes each command to the path that corresponds to the region in which the specified data addresses fall. For example, Figure 5-6 illustrates the policy for a device with two paths. In this example, DMP routes commands that specify starting block addresses between 00 and 03 on path 0, those that specify addresses between 04 and 07 to path 1, those that specify addresses between 08 and 11 to path 0, and so forth. (The four-block divisor is artificially low for graphic simplicity; DMP's actual default divisor is 2048 blocks, or one megabyte.)

Figure 5-6 I/O path selection with the balanced path routing policy

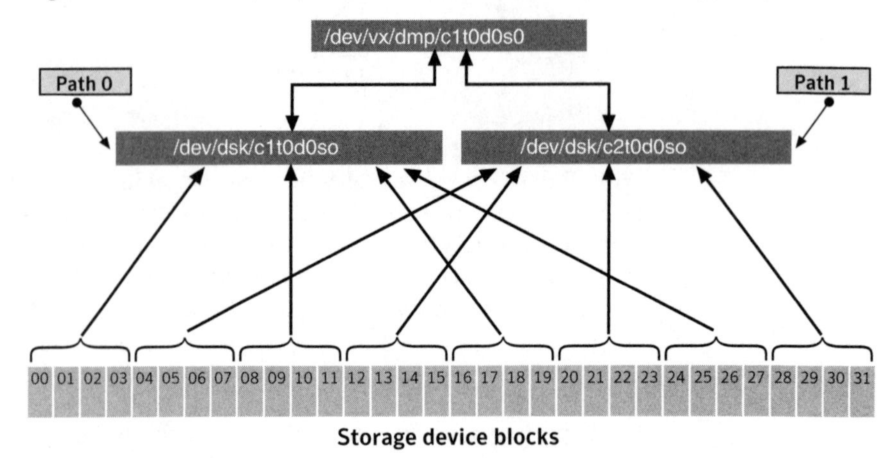

The balanced path policy is DMP's default policy for LUNs presented by active-active arrays. It is particularly beneficial for high-speed sequential reading from LUNs and dual-port disk drives with read-ahead cache.

Round-robin routing

The round-robin I/O request routing policy issues approximately equal numbers of commands on each active path. The round-robin policy is usually optimal when most I/O requests to a device specify approximately the same amount of data transfer, and in storage networks whose loading is relatively evenly distributed.

Minimum queue length routing

The minimum queue length policy routes each command on the active path with the smallest number of outstanding commands. This policy tends to counteract momentary load imbalances, as for example, when there is a bottleneck on a path due to error recovery or overload from other LUNs.

Adaptive routing

Adaptive routing allows DMP to route commands based on path priorities that it calculates periodically based on recent throughput, favoring those whose throughput has been highest. DMP routes commands in proportion to paths' relative priorities. For example, if there are three active paths whose priorities have been calculated to be 3, 2, and 1 respectively, half of all incoming requests are routed to path 1, a third to path 2, and the remaining sixth to path 3. As I/O load on a higher priority path increases, it tends to deliver lower throughput, resulting in a lower priority on the next recalculation.

The adaptive routing policy tends to optimize throughput for rapidly varying I/O loads, such as database applications that include both transactions (short transfers) and periodic table scans (long transfers). It is also useful in storage networks where different paths have discernibly different average performance, such as long-distance paths with different numbers of network "hops" or individual links of different speeds.

Priority routing

As with the adaptive routing policy, priority routing assigns commands to paths based on path priorities. With this policy, however, path priorities are assigned by administrators, and only change by administrative action. The priority routing policy allows administrators to assign path priorities based on considerations other than performance, such as applications' relative importance to an enterprise.

Single active path (preferred path) routing

As its name implies, the single active path policy routes all commands on one path, called the preferred path. Only if the preferred path fails does DMP route commands to a secondary one. The single active path policy is normally used with active-passive arrays that can only support I/O to each LUN on one path at a time.

Using DMP when other path managers are present

Path managers that are functionally similar to DMP are available from some disk array and system vendors. There are three principal differences between DMP and the path managers typically supplied by hardware vendors:

- Typically, hardware vendors' path managers are optimized to support the vendor's own products, sometimes to the exclusion of other vendors' storage and systems. VxVM on the other hand is inherently heterogeneous, both with respect to platforms and storage devices, and in its ability to intermix different types of storage in a single virtual device configuration.

- VxVM is more closely integrated with the VxFS file system and with major database managers than is typical for hardware vendor-supplied virtualization and path management software. Integration with adjacent layers in the I/O software stack tends to minimize administrative complexity, and therefore cost.
- Vendor-supplied path managers are typically extra-cost adjuncts to disk arrays, whereas DMP is an integral part of VxVM.

For a variety of reasons, other path managers are sometimes present on systems where DMP is installed. Both approaches have their own benefits and limitations. To manage systems in which two path managers are present, administrators should appreciate how DMP and other path managers interact with each other.

Path manager operation

Multipath management further enhances data availability and I/O performance. Path [3] in Figure 5-2 represents an I/O software stack that includes a path manager such as DMP. In this scenario:

- The virtualization layer transforms each request to a virtual volume into one or more commands which it issues to metadevices that represent disk drives or LUNs.
- The path management layer issues each metadevice command to a single operating system device, representing a specific access path to the actual disk drive or LUN.

No value is gained by performing the second transformation more than once; that is, by having two path managers operating. Generally, path managers are unaware of each other, and therefore do not coordinate the commands they issue. More importantly, they do not coordinate their respective error recovery actions.

Typically, path managers can be enabled or disabled either on a per-device basis or system-wide. By default, VxVM manages all devices that it recognizes as disks or LUNs, including controlling access paths to them. VxVM path management for a device can be disabled by administrative command.

DMP coexistence with other path managers

Because all path managers perform essentially the same function, all behave in essentially the same way. They create some form of metanodes to represent the devices they control, and redirect commands addressed to the metanodes to an operating system driver node representing an actual device. To guarantee that they control all access to devices, some path managers suppress operating system device nodes so that they do not appear to DMP as though they represent storage devices.

Path-suppressing path managers

Path managers that suppress device paths do so in one of two ways:

- They suppress all but one operating system device node for each device they control. Path managers that do this use unsuppressed paths as metanodes for the devices they represent.
- They completely replace operating system device nodes that represent paths to devices they control with their own metanodes. Path managers that do this typically name their metanodes in some readily-identifiable way.

Both of these techniques effectively suppress all but one path to each device. DMP's metanodes (as illustrated in Figure 5-5) can link to a path-suppressing path manager's metanodes, but because they appear to be single-path devices, DMP performs no useful function.

Non-suppressing path managers

Other path managers do not suppress the operating system device tree nodes for the devices they control. Non-suppressing path managers leave operating system nodes for the devices they control unmodified. They represent metadevices in one of two ways:

- They add their metanodes to the operating system device tree.
- They place their metanodes in a separate file system directory. Vendors of this type of path manager have been slow to provide APIs that would allow DMP to determine relationships between metanodes and operating system device nodes, so historically, DMP has had difficulty coexisting with them, although this situation is changing.

Table 5-1 lists path suppression characteristics of common path managers.

Table 5-1 Path suppression characteristics of common path managers

Path Manager	Vendor	Type	Platforms
ATF (Automatic Transparent Failover)	EMC Corporation	Path suppressing	Solaris

Table 5-1 Path suppression characteristics of common path managers *(continued)*

Path Manager	Vendor	Type	Platforms
RDAC (Redundant Disk Array Controller)	IBM Corporation	Path suppressing	Solaris AIX
STMS	Sun Microsystems	Path suppressing	Solaris
SDD (called VPATH on AIX platform)	IBM Corporation	Non- suppressing	Solaris
PowerPath (Native mode)	EMC Corporation	Non- suppressing	Solaris HP-UX Linux
PowerPath (Pseudo mode)	EMC Corporation	Non- suppressing	Solaris

Unless prevented from doing so, DMP discovers both operating system nodes and metanodes of non-suppressing path managers. Both path managers might attempt to manage access to the same devices, with obvious conflicts. To avoid this, administrators can declare devices to be foreign to VxVM. DMP does not control access paths to foreign devices, but the VxVM virtualization layer can still add them to disk groups and use them as volume components.

A coexistence example

EMC Corporation's PowerPath software is frequently found on systems where DMP is installed. PowerPath operates either in pseudo device mode (also called emcpower mode) or in native device mode, both of which are non-path suppressing.

PowerPath pseudo-device mode

In pseudo-device mode, PowerPath creates metanodes that are conceptually similar to DMP's for each device it controls. Figure 5-7 illustrates the two paths through the I/O software stack in a system with both DMP and pseudo-device mode PowerPath installed.

Figure 5-7 DMP with EMC PowerPath in pseudo-device mode

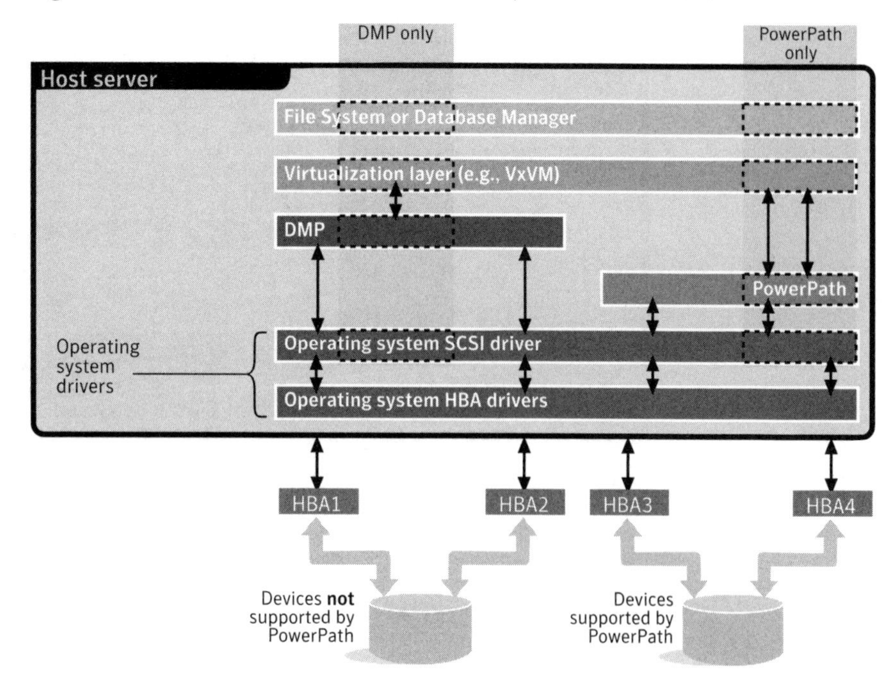

Operating system nodes for pseudo-device mode PowerPath are visible in the device tree. DMP does not recognize PowerPath pseudo-devices, but it will recognize and attempt to control the corresponding operating system nodes unless they are declared foreign. EMC Corporation provides scripts that declare PowerPath-controlled devices to be foreign to VxVM.

PowerPath native mode

Primarily for compatibility with existing applications and scripts, PowerPath also operates in native mode on certain platforms (Table 5-1). Applications and scripts address disk drives and LUNs controlled by native mode PowerPath by their operating system names, so they work without modification.

In native mode, PowerPath does not create metanodes. Instead, it directs each I/O command to an operating system node according to its load balancing policy, regardless of which node originally received the I/O request. If DMP were to control a PowerPath native mode device, as suggested by the polygon labeled "DMP and PowerPath" in Figure 5-8, VxVM virtualization layer commands might reach target devices on different paths than the ones on which they were issued.

Figure 5-8 DMP with EMC PowerPath in native mode

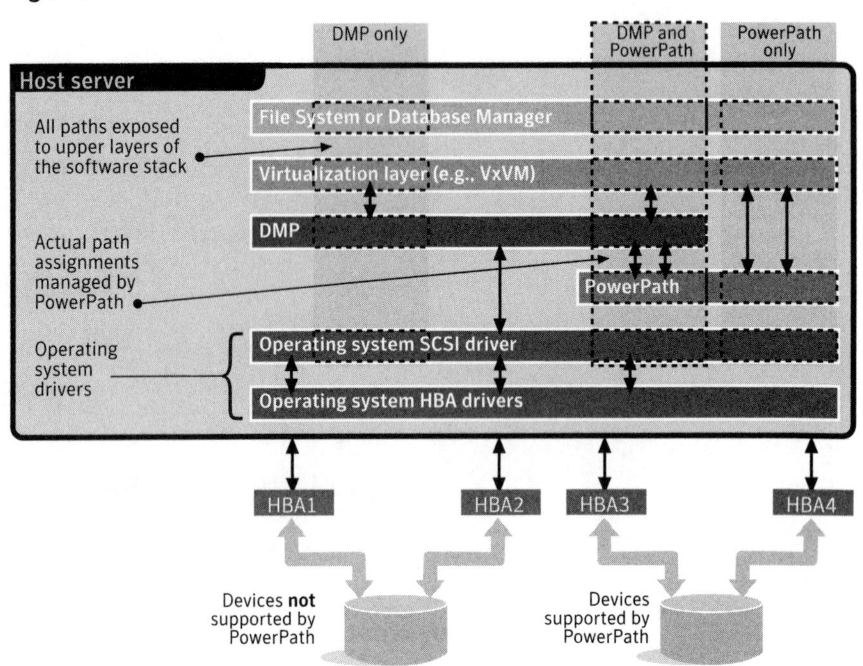

If PowerPath is the only path manager in the stack, its I/O request re-routing is immaterial to the virtualization layer. But if DMP also attempts to manage paths, PowerPath may re-route DMP's commands, possibly affecting I/O performance adversely. Worse, DMP and PowerPath error recovery are almost certain to conflict, with unpredictable results.

DMP and native mode PowerPath have been used successfully in Veritas cluster applications. Veritas clusters use SCSI persistent group reservations (PGRs) to prevent so-called split brain behavior when the connection between two servers breaks. DMP propagates PGR requests on all paths to a device. With native mode PowerPath, all device paths are visible to DMP, so PGR request propagation is possible.

Summarizing Dynamic Multi-pathing

Effective management of multiple access paths to storage devices keeps data available to applications when storage network components fail. For disk arrays that support concurrent access to LUNs on multiple paths, balancing I/O load across two or more paths can also improve I/O performance. To be effective, path management must be automatic, and load balancing must be consistent with data center policy.

The Storage Foundation Dynamic Multi-pathing facility automates both path failover and I/O load balancing with policies that can help achieve a variety of I/O performance goals.

Disk arrays may be active-active, supporting concurrent access to LUNs through two or more controllers, or they may be active-passive, supporting access to each LUN through a single controller at any instant. Active-passive arrays may support concurrent access on two or more paths. In active-passive arrays, failover may be implicit (caused by issuing I/O commands on secondary paths) or explicit (caused by array-specific commands). Disk arrays may fail LUNs over from primary paths to secondary ones individually or in groups.

Major system and storage vendors offer path management software, usually to manage access paths for their own products. Vendor-supplied path management software can co-exist with DMP in a system, but configurations in which both attempt to manage the same devices should generally be avoided. In most cases, DMP and vendor-supplied path management software should manage path access for different sets of devices.

DMP can control more different types of devices than typical vendor-supplied software. Additionally, it implements a more comprehensive set of I/O load balancing policies. In general, DMP specifications are technically superior to those of most vendor-supplied path managers, but care should be used in removing any path management software from a system, because unpredictable results may occur.

Chapter 6

A closer look at the Storage Foundation: the Storage Foundation Management Server

This chapter includes the following topics:

- Single-point storage management
- Resource management with SFMS
- SFMS resource groups
- Alert monitoring
- Storage Foundation Management Server services
- Locating specific Storage Foundation objects
- Summarizing the Storage Foundation Management Server

Single-point storage management

Both the VxVM volume manager and the VxFS file system provide central management of all online storage and data resources controlled by a single Storage Foundation host, either through the Veritas Enterprise Administrator graphical console or through scriptable command line interfaces. As data centers acquire more servers and storage resources, however, and as storage moves from within the server out onto the network, individual application and database servers become inadequate focal points for storage management. Increasingly, enterprises need a holistic view of their storage and data so, for example, they can assess utilization on a data center-wide basis, or so they can take management actions whose effect may transcend a single server or application without causing unintended adverse side effects.

The Storage Foundation Management Server (SFMS)

The Storage Foundation Management Server (SFMS), introduced with Version 5 of the Storage Foundation, answers the need for a data center-wide view of storage and data. The Storage Foundation Management Server is a browser-based client-server application that manages Storage Foundation resources (disks, volumes, file systems, and other related resources) for any number of management clients (application and database servers) in the data center. Figure 6-1 illustrates the positioning of SFMS in a multi-server data center.

Figure 6-1 Storage Foundation Management Server in the data center

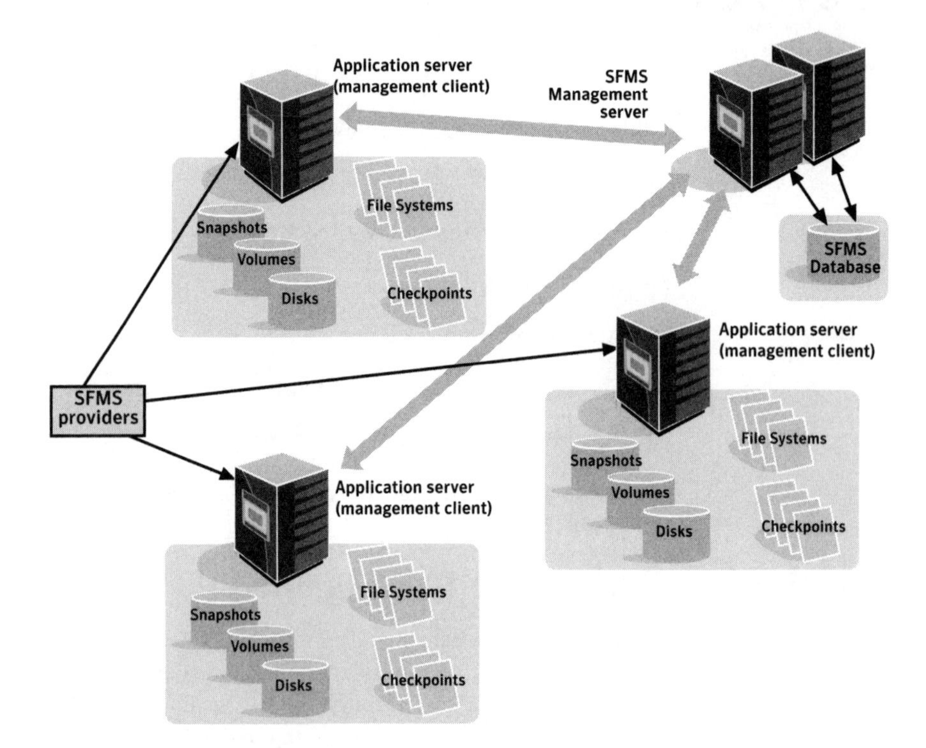

Figure 6-1 shows multiple application servers (called management clients in SFMS terminology) equipped with SFMS provider software. SFMS Providers discover

Storage Foundation resources on the servers on which they run and report their state to a central server that runs Storage Foundation Management Server software. The SFMS server maintains a database of Storage Foundation resource state information for all management clients to which it is connected. Providers update the SFMS server's state information whenever changes occur on their local servers.

SFMS software may run on a dedicated system or in an application or database server that is also an SFMS client. The SFMS server may be configured as a Veritas Cluster Server Application Service Group so that failure of the system on which it is running leaves central storage management services intact.

Administrators interact with an SFMS server via a browser. Authorized administrators can authenticate themselves to SFMS and manage Storage Foundation resources from any browser-equipped system that has a network connection to the management server.

Because it maintains a central repository of information about all Storage Foundation resources in the data center, an SFMS server is uniquely positioned to perform four important functions from an overall data center perspective:

- Managing Storage Foundation resources
- Reporting on the state of Storage Foundation resources across the data center
- Monitoring and responding to alerts related to Storage Foundation resources
- Performing common and user-defined Storage Foundation related services

The sections that follow discuss these functions in more detail.

Resource management with SFMS

In a data center with many storage resources it can be difficult to obtain an overall picture of how well data center storage is performing–which resources are functioning properly, which have faulted, and which are at risk because some redundant component has failed. Without a comprehensive picture of what's going on, it is difficult for an administrator to make informed decisions and take optimal actions that may affect resources other than those that are acted upon directly.

Administrators do have the option of using server-based management tools, including Storage Foundation tools, to collect information about the state of Storage Foundation resources on a server-by-server basis. But with dozens or even hundreds of servers in a data center, monitoring resource state information for each one individually and consolidating and correlating information by hand is impractical.

The Storage Foundation Management Server resource management facility collects, stores, consolidates, and presents state information for all Storage Foundation resources (disks, volumes, snapshots, file systems, Storage Checkpoints, and so forth) in a variety of useful views. Additionally, it provides a single console from which management actions on user-defined groups of Storage Foundation resources can be initiated.

SFMS uses a web browser-based user interface to present information in a layered form, starting with the concise dashboard view shown in Figure 6-2. The dashboard view, presented upon login, contains highly summarized information about all managed storage, server, and application resources at a glance. Graphics and color coding are both used to quickly draw an administrator's attention to resources that require attention because they are either faulted (not functioning) or are at risk (configured to be fault-tolerant, but having one or more failed components that could result in faulting if a further component failure occurs).

Figure 6-2 Storage Foundation Management Server managing dashboard

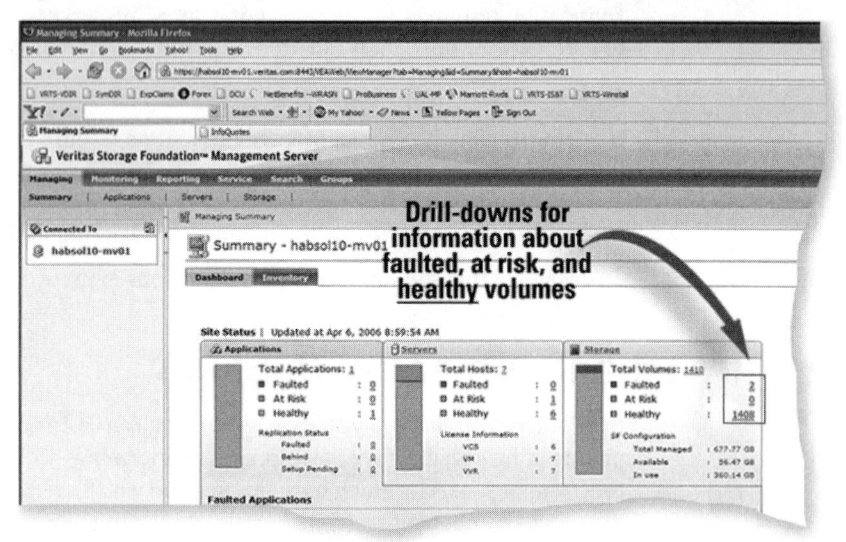

Starting with this dashboard view, an administrator can drill down to view information about specific servers, storage devices, file systems, network connections, and other Storage Foundation resources. For example, the arrow in Figure 6-2 highlights hot links to SFMS pages that display information about VxVM volumes on management client systems. Separate links allow administrators to move immediately to views that present information about faulted, at-risk, and healthy volumes.

Figure 6-3 illustrates how quickly an administrator can isolate a problem with an example of three stages of drill-down to increasingly more detailed information.

The browser window labeled `[1]` in Figure 6-3, reached by clicking the `Faulted` link indicated by the arrow in Figure 6-2, presents a table of information about faulted VxVM volumes and volume sets on servers managed by SFMS server `habsansol10-mv01`. In this table, as in all SFMS displays, managed objects such as the volumes themselves (left-most column), the hosts that control them, and the disk groups to which they belong, are all represented by hot links, so that by clicking any one of them, an administrator can immediately display more detailed information.

For example, the window labeled `[2]` in Figure 6-3, reached by clicking the name of faulted volume `concat_vol_3`, drills down to overview information about the volume. Clicking one of the other two tabs in the window takes the administrator to displays of disk or snapshot information for the volume respectively. Clicking the `Administer` link in window `[2]` displays the window labeled `[3]` in Figure 6-3. This window presents information about the disk(s) that comprise the volume, including name, layout, status, total capacity, and capacity currently available for allocation. In addition, a drop-down list of available commands, indicated by the arrowhead in window `[3]` makes it easy for an administrator to take immediate corrective action.

Figure 6-3 Storage Foundation Management Server drill-down

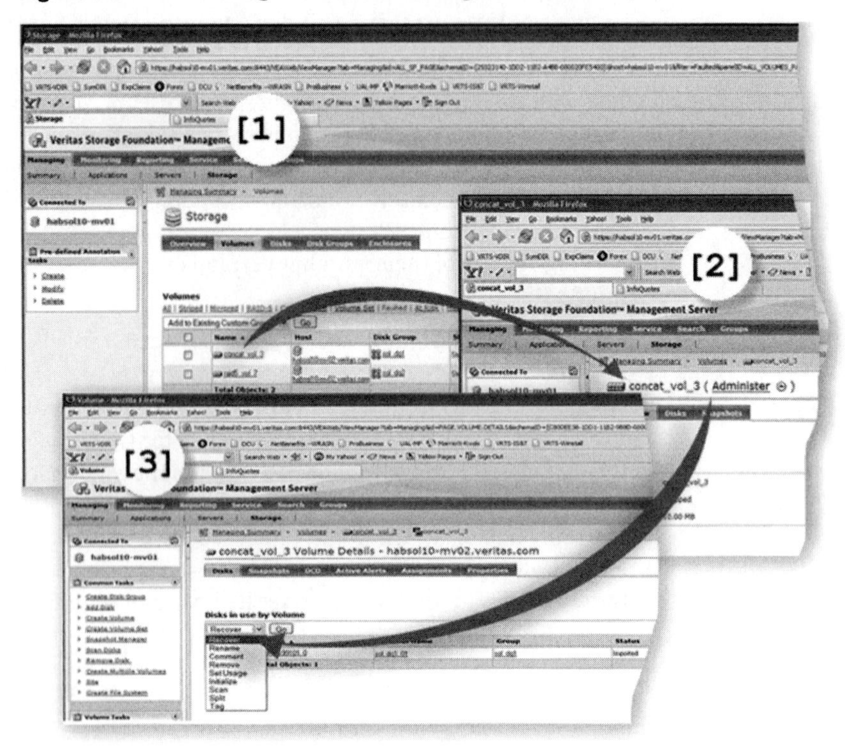

Thus, with a few mouse clicks an administrator can move rapidly from an overview of data center storage to pinpointing a specific storage object for which administrative action might be required, and initiate that action on the server that controls the object. This sequence illustrates some general principles of the Storage Foundation Management Server:

- Rapid drill-down from overview to specific information—in the example of Figure 6-3, three clicks is all that is required to get to the point of issuing a remedial command.
- Flexible navigation—in any window, all managed objects are displayed as hot links to which an administrator can navigate instantly with a single click.
- User-friendly ordering—any tabular display produced by SFMS can be sorted on any column, thus allowing the administrator to decide what attributes of a view are most appropriate to the situation.
- Instant switchover from monitoring to active management—SFMS windows that display actionable objects include `Administer` hot links that lead to

windows from commands in a drop-down list can be executed on the selected object.

Thus, SFMS makes it easy to gain an overview of the state of data center storage, while at the same time providing an ability to drill down to isolate and repair individual problems. The browser-based graphical user interface obviates the need for administrators to memorize either command syntax or the interrelationships of Storage Foundation objects.

Using SFMS to view information

SFMS presents the information it monitors in several different views, so that specialists whose primary concerns are storage, networks, file systems, databases, servers, clusters, applications, or even arbitrary user-defined groups of Storage Foundation resources, can instantly view exactly the information that is of concern to them.

For each type of resource about which it displays information, SFMS includes filters for common sub-categories. For example, when viewing information about disks, with a single click, an administrator can filter the display to include:

- All disks under management
- Healthy disks (disks with no faults), whether part of a VxVM disk group or not
- Offline disks (disks that are not faulted, but are not available for configuration)
- Disks discovered on managed systems that have not been initialized by VxVM
- Disks initialized by VxVM that are not part of a volume or disk group (free disks)
- Other disks that do not fit into any of these categories

Similarly, when viewing information about VxVM volumes, an administrator can selectively view:

- All volumes under management
- Striped, RAID-5, mirrored or concatenated volumes only
- Healthy, faulted, or at-risk volumes only

These filters provide instant access to data center-wide views of storage allocation that can be used for a variety of purposes. For example:

- Quickly identifying disks and volumes that have failed, and are presumably impacting application availability
- Quickly identifying volumes that are configured to be fault-tolerant, but which are currently at risk due to redundant component failure

- Obtaining an overview of how storage is provisioned across the data center (for example, how much is mirrored and what systems it is connected to)
- Obtaining an overview of free space in file systems across the data center

In addition to built-in filters, SFMS provides administrators with an ability to group resources according to any business-related criteria and quickly view the properties and status of resources in a group. SFMS resource groups are discussed later in this chapter.

SFMS active management operations

SFMS displays are deliberately designed to be very regular, to minimize initial training, memorization, and re-familiarization requirements. Information is presented in tabular form, with the left-most column of each table containing the names of displayed objects, and the remaining columns representing object properties. Above each tabular listing is a drop-down list of actions that can be taken on the type of object displayed. For example, Figure 6-4 illustrates the actions that can be taken on VxVM volume objects.

Figure 6-4 Active management actions in SFMS

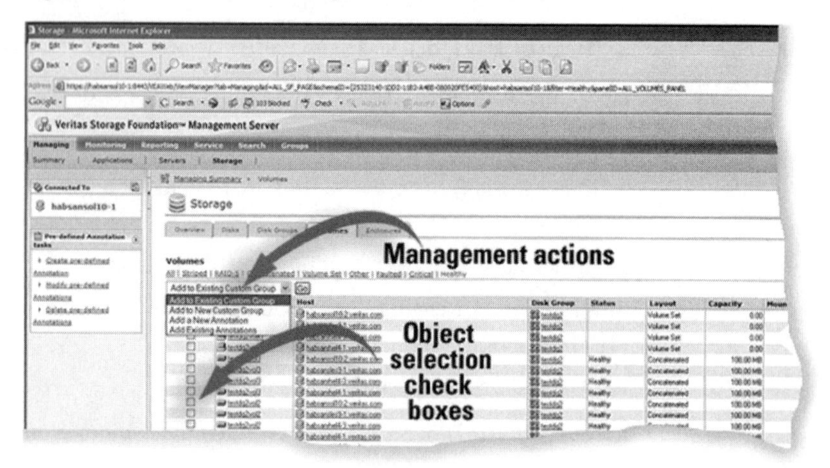

To the left of the object name column in Figure 6-4 is a column of check boxes used to select objects. To actively manage one or more objects from the SFMS console, an administrator checks the box corresponding to each object, selects the action to be taken from the drop-down list, and clicks the Go button, launching a wizard that is used to specify any parameters necessary to perform the action. When the wizard has collected the required parameters, SFMS cooperates with the host that owns each object as necessary to perform the indicated operation on the object. For example, as Figure 6-4 illustrates, the management actions that SFMS can take on VxVM volumes are:

- Adding the selected volume to a new or existing grouping of managed objects
- Annotating the selected volume with an arbitrary character string

SFMS groups are discussed in a following section. Annotations are named character strings that can be attached to objects' records in the SFMS database for informational purposes. Annotation names and values are both completely at administrative discretion. They can be used for persistent recording of any useful information about Storage Foundation resources:

- An annotation named `Creator` might be used to record the name of the administrator who created a disk group or volume.
- An annotation named `Intent` might be used to record the original purpose for which a disk group was created.
- An annotation named `History` might be used to record a repurposed disk's prior disk group membership.

In all of these cases, the value assigned to the annotation is completely at the administrator's discretion, so, for example, responsible administrators' names or employee numbers could be supplied as values for an annotation named `Creator`.

For some objects, attaching an annotation may result in SFMS taking additional action on the object itself. For example, an annotation attached to a VxVM volume becomes a tag used by the Dynamic Storage Tiering (DST) facility. (Volume tags are discussed in Storage tiers and placement classes .) Figure 6-5 illustrates the use of SFMS management operations to annotate (assign tags to) volumes for use by the DST facility.

Figure 6-5 Using SFMS to assign volume tags for Dynamic Storage Tiering

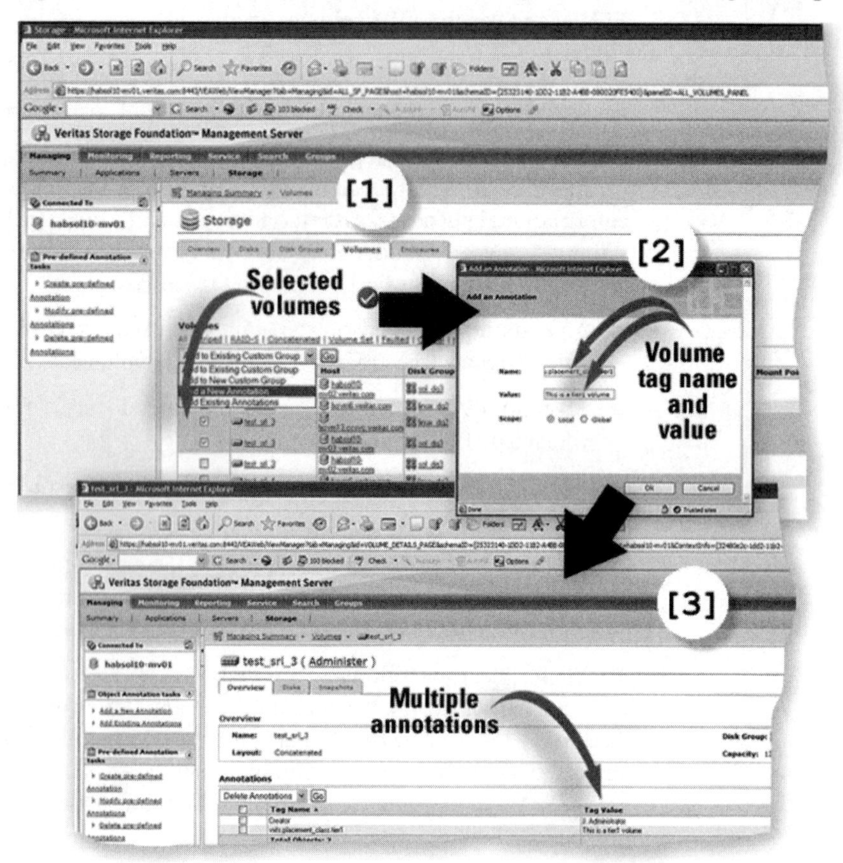

The display labeled `[1]` in Figure 6-5 illustrates the selection of multiple volumes to which an annotation is to be applied. Selecting the `Add New Annotation` command and clicking the `Go` button invokes the wizard panel labeled `[2]` in the figure. The DST facility recognizes volume tag names in the form `vxfs_placement_class`.classname, where classname is the name of the volume's placement class or storage tier (`tier1` in the example). DST does not use the tag value, so it is available for use as an informative comment. In the example, the `Local` radio button is clicked, causing the annotation to be sent to the host that controls the volume for assignment as well as being stored in the SFMS database. Clicking OK performs the action. The display labeled `[3]` drills down to the `test_srl_3` volume to illustrate that the volume tag annotation has been added to a `Creator` annotation that had already been applied to the volume for another purpose.

SFMS resource groups

Authorized administrators can use SFMS to view the state of the resources they control, whether those resources are associated with one application server or many. They can quickly determine which resources have failed and why, and so begin to take informed corrective action.

SFMS not only reports failed resources, but also at-risk ones—failure-tolerant resources that are functioning, but are at risk of failing due to the failure of some component that comprises them. For example, a VxVM volume whose component disks are configured to have two or more access paths becomes at-risk if one of its disks is reduced to a single available access path. Likewise, a RAID-5 or mirrored volume with a failed disk, or a multi-volume VxFS file system with an unavailable data-only volume becomes at-risk, even though it is still functional. Armed with information about at-risk resources, an administrator can take corrective action, for example, by repairing a failed network link or replacing a failed disk, thus forestalling outages that might result if additional component failures occurred.

The resource monitoring facility of SFMS extends the scope of administrative specialists in the data center. For example, a single administrator might be responsible for:

- One or more servers or clusters
- One or more disk groups, independent of the servers with which they are associated
- A group of file systems or databases on one or more servers
- An arbitrary collection of Storage Foundation resources that comprise an application or other business organizational unit

SFMS includes facilities that provide for grouping arbitrary sets of resources and monitoring and reporting on the group's state. The SFMS dashboard shown in Figure 6-2 provides an overview of group state, and allows an administrator to monitor and manage the resources in individual groups.

SFMS supports two types of resource groups—application groups and custom groups. For application groups, SFMS tracks relationships among resources, and adds resources to or removes them from groups as appropriate. For example, if an application group includes a Storage Foundation disk group, SFMS automatically makes any disks that are added to the disk group part of the application group. Application groups may be defined by users, or they may be auto-discovered by Storage Foundation components such as the Veritas Volume Replicator (VVR) or the Database Editions. On command, these components create application groups and add all appropriate resources to them, so that administrators are not required to remember which resources should be in these types of groups. Creating a VVR or database group creates a view of exactly the

Storage Foundation resources used by the group, providing a complete picture of the group's state without distraction from other resources that are not relevant to its operation.

To avoid automatic addition and deletion of subordinate resources in a group, administrators can create custom groups. Custom groups are also views of selected sets of resources, but unlike application groups, they do not make assumptions about resource interrelationships. For example, if a disk is added to a VxVM disk group that is part of a custom resource group, the disk does not automatically become part of the custom group. Custom groups are useful for monitoring resources that may share underlying objects, such as a set of volumes in a disk group that also exports volumes that are not part of the custom group.

Resource reporting

A large data center may have hundreds of file systems and thousands of volumes, disks, and storage network access paths. Simply keeping track of Storage Foundation resources and their levels of utilization can be a significant task. And yet the more complex a data center, the more important it becomes to have a global view of storage resource allocation and utilization.

For example, most large enterprises purchase online storage in bulk on annual or other periodic schedules. When it's time to plan the next purchase, considerable effort is typically devoted to determining how much storage is needed, based on users' estimates of their anticipated requirements. But analyst report upon analyst report shows that enterprise storage utilization can be quite low. Users sometimes project that they will need additional storage because it is too onerous for them to analyze how well they are utilizing the storage they have and plan how to redeploy excess capacity.

Another important question, especially for data centers that operate many small single-application servers, is the state of readiness of storage and data resources. Data centers with many single-application servers count on being able to pool storage devices and servers and to deploy them upon demand. For deployments to succeed, resources must be available, fully operational, and possibly even pre-configured.

Storage Foundation Management Server reports provide instant information of the operating state and utilization of Storage Foundation file systems, volumes, disks, network paths, databases, and servers. As with the monitoring function, data center-wide overview information is presented in dashboard form, with the capability of "drilling down" to observe the individual resource level if necessary. Figure 6-6 illustrates the SFMS reporting home page.

Figure 6-6 SFMS usage reporting home page

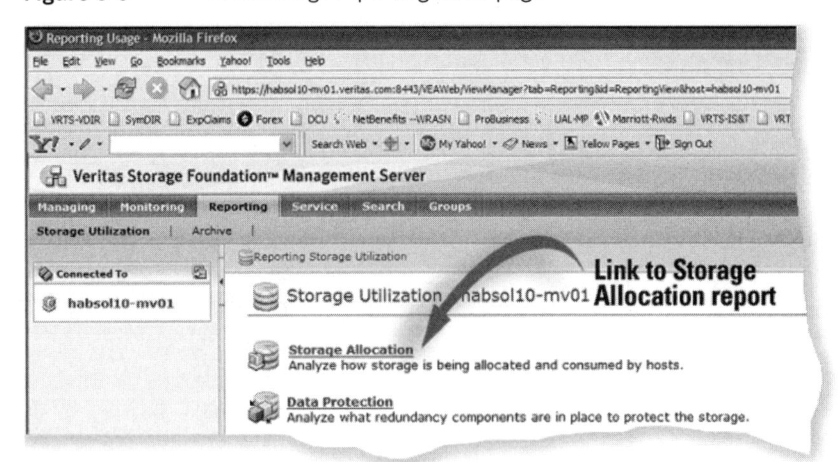

As Figure 6-6 suggests, SFMS provides reports on:

- The amount of storage managed by VxVM
- Utilization of file systems on VxVM volumes
- The amount of storage capacity protected against data loss by mirroring and RAID5 and against corruption by snapshots

For example, Figure 6-7 illustrates the Storage Utilization summary report displayed when the link indicated in Figure 6-6 is clicked. The pie chart summarizes the usage of all storage on managed hosts in terms of whether or not it is managed by VxVM, and if so, whether or not it is part of a VxVM volume. An administrator might use this chart to quickly determine the total amount of storage that is available for use in the entire data center, for example.

The bar charts list the hosts with the most storage capacity not managed by VxVM and the most VxVM-managed storage not being exported as volumes. Clicking any of the bars causes a list of the selected host's storage Allocation Summary report to be displayed. These reports might be used, for example, to quickly direct an administrator to servers from which unused storage could be reclaimed, or to determine whether storage must be provisioned to a host before additional volumes can be created and exported.

Figure 6-7 An SFMS summary report (Storage Allocation)

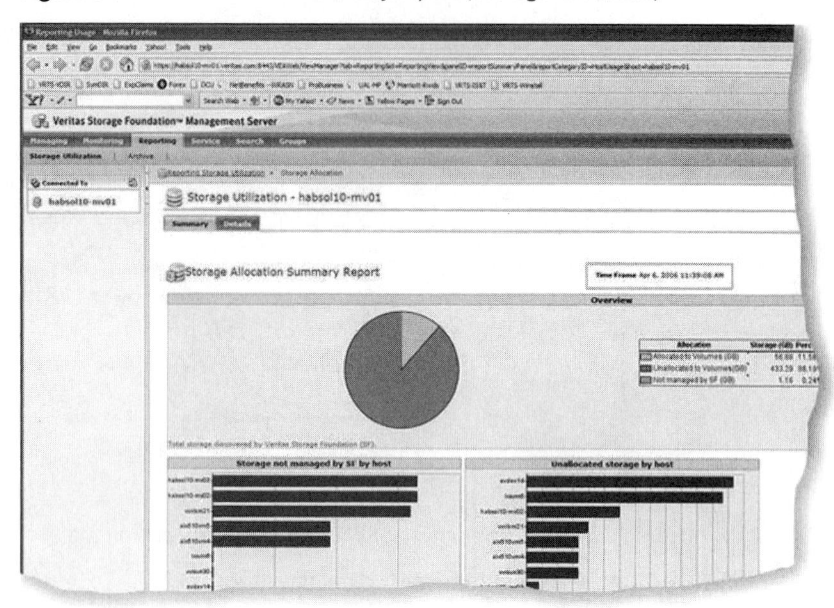

From reporting to active management

SFMS reporting is designed to permit an administrator to quickly survey the state of storage across a data center, zero in on potential issues, and switch quickly from a passive observation mode to an active management mode. The unique value of SFMS is that it provides this facility for all of the managed hosts and Storage Foundation objects in a data center from a single location.

For example, clicking on the bar indicated in Figure 6-7 results in displaying overview information for host `habsol10-mv03`. Two additional clicks result in the display shown in Figure 6-8, from which administrative commands, such as the highlighted `Create File System`, can be issued to one or more selected volumes.

Each administrative command invokes a wizard that leads an administrator through the steps required to perform the selected function. For example, Figure 6-8 illustrates the first and last panels of the `Create File System` wizard, which is used to create a file system on the selected volume.

This example is indicative of the Storage Foundation Management Server reporting user interface style. The key characteristics common to all SFMS reports are:

- Beginning with a data center-wide view of objects of interest, rapid drill-down to areas of probable interest (example: one-click to view host with largest number of volumes containing no file system)

- One-click transition from report views to active management views from which actions can be taken on selected objects (example: two clicks from host overview to view for active administration of volumes)
- Comprehensive guidance through the steps required to perform administrative actions (example: wizard panels to provide all information and options required to create a file system)

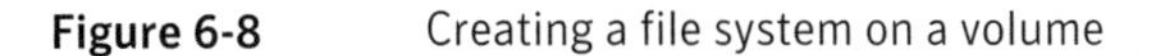

Figure 6-8 Creating a file system on a volume

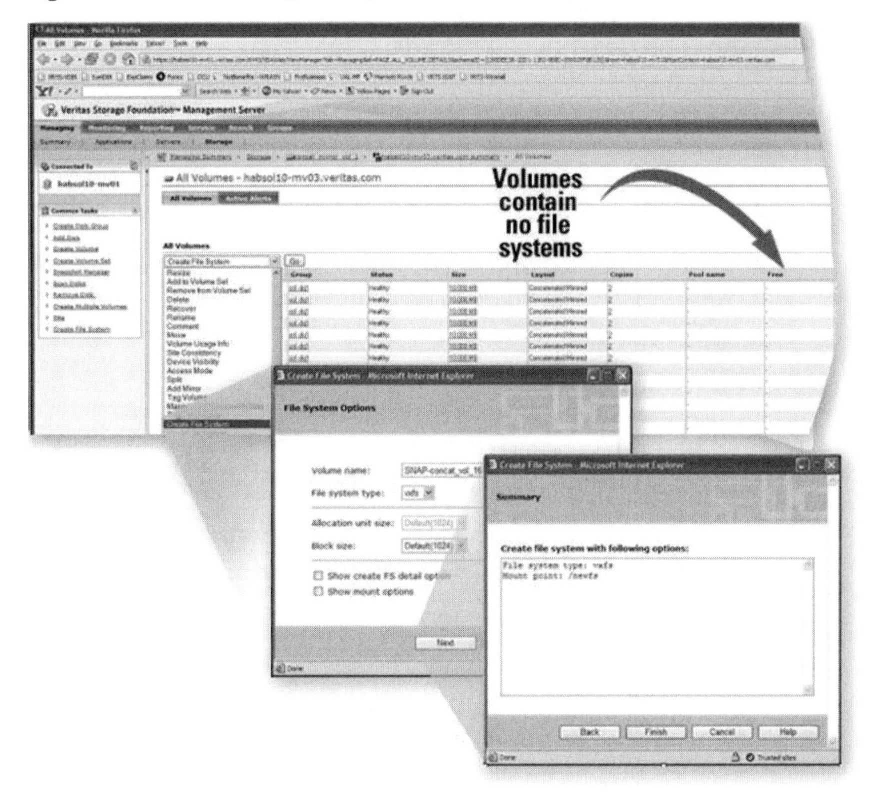

This demonstrates how SFMS reporting expands the scope of administrative control by presenting a comprehensive picture of storage in the data center from which issues can be quickly identified and needed management actions taken.

Alert monitoring

An important part of effective storage management in a complex data center is recognition of and reaction to exceptional conditions that arise. Disk, storage network, application, and other events that might require management action, must be detected, their locations isolated, their causes and severity assessed, and responses made, in the context of a data center that may contain thousands of managed objects.

The providers that run in SFMS-managed application and database servers solve this problem by reporting Storage Foundation alerts to the central SFMS server. The SFMS server console's `Monitoring` tab displays an overview of the state of managed objects across the data center. Figure 6-9 shows a progression of views from data center-wide overview to individual alert raised against a single resource. Again, within two clicks, the administrator is led from a global view of the data center's state to a pinpoint description of the precise problem.

Figure 6-9 SFMS alert summary and detail pages

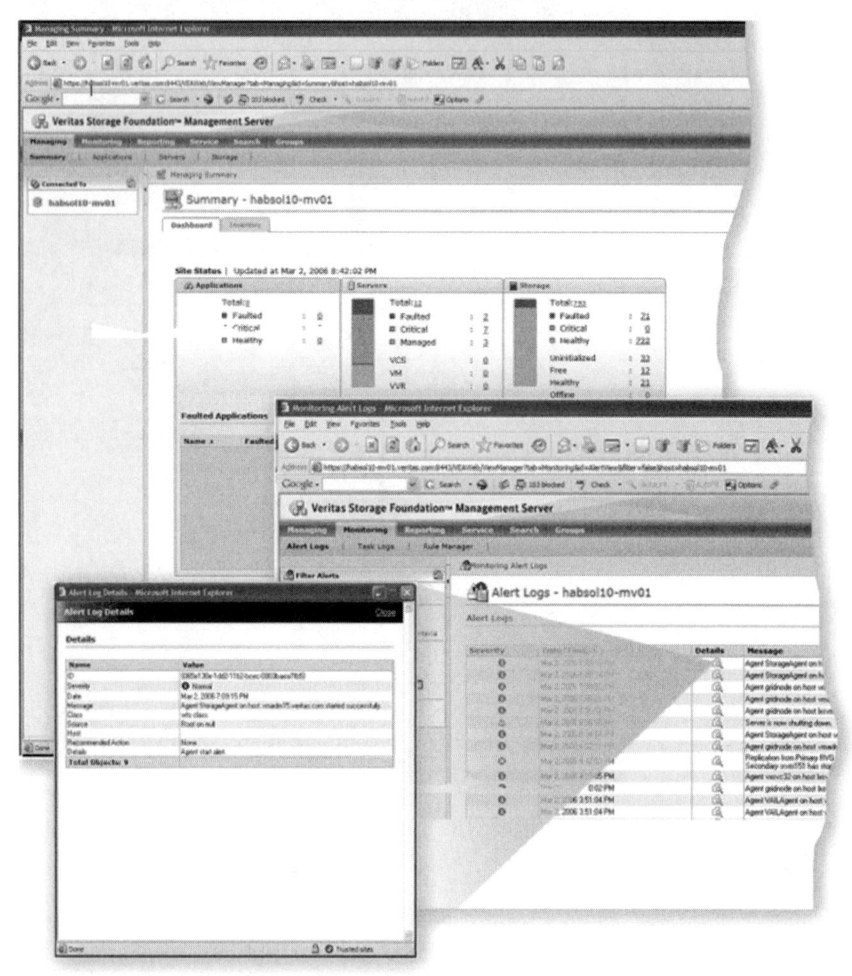

Storage Foundation Management Server services

The Storage Foundation Management Server centralizes and simplifies certain common storage management services by providing wizards that ensure the services are defined completely and optionally store them in the SFMS database for later execution. SFMS includes wizards for creating and storing service definitions for:

- All Dynamic Storage Tiering functions, including file placement policy creation, assignment, deletion, modification, and display
- Migration of data between two VxVM volumes, useful, for example, for moving data from older disk arrays to newer ones that will replace them without application downtime
- Transferring control of a disk group from one host to another
- Modifying dynamic multi-pathing (DMP—Chapter 5) configurations and verifying that existing configurations meet administrative intent for connectivity

In addition to these services, SFMS enables administrators to define custom services, arbitrary lists of commands that are pre-stored in the SFMS database and executed whenever required. The SFMS Service Builder page shown in Figure 6-10, which is reached from the SFMS `Service` tab, is the starting point for creating pre-defined services.

Figure 6-10 SFMS service builder start page

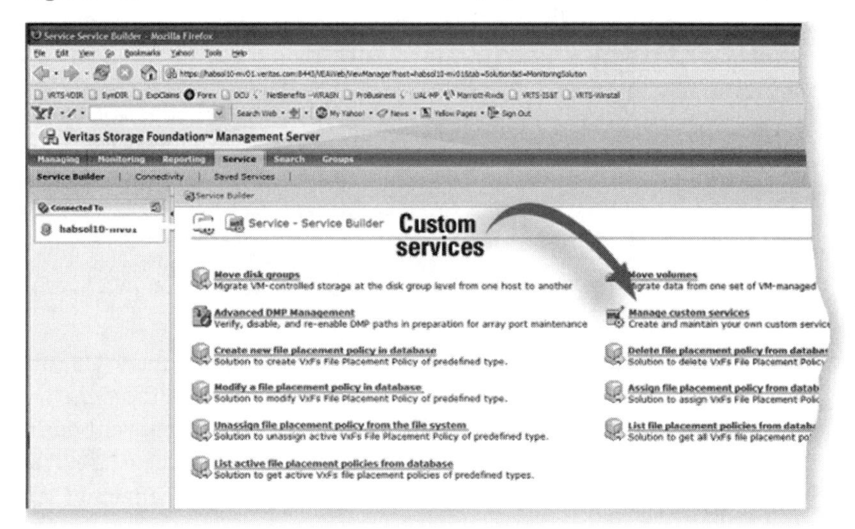

Clicking any of the eleven service definition types on this page invokes a wizard that is specific to the type of service represented. Each wizard guides an administrator through creation of the service, ensuring that all required parameters are supplied for syntactic correctness. At the end of the service creation phase, a service definition may be saved in the SFMS database for later execution, and may optionally be executed immediately.

The `Manage Custom Services` link indicated in Figure 6-10 provides the mechanism by which administrators can define their own services in the form of scripts of console commands. Like the other links on this page, `Manage Custom Services` guides an administrator through creation of the commands that comprise a service. It saves the completed service definition in the SFMS database, and optionally executes it. This facility makes it possible for administrators to pre-define any common sequence of management operations, store the definition, and invoke the service whenever circumstances require it.

For example, an administrator might define a custom service to defragment the file systems on all web servers in the data center and store it in the database. The service might be invoked periodically (for example, every Saturday night, or it might be executed whenever a particularly intense set of web page updates might have left file systems more fragmented than is optimal for performance.

Figure 6-11 SFMS service execution and maintenance page

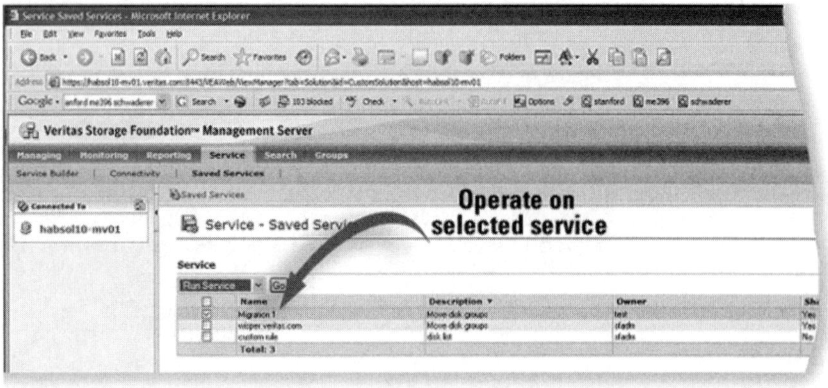

Once a service has been defined and stored in the SFMS database, it can be invoked from the `Saved Services` page reached from the `Service` navigation tab. Figure 6-11 illustrates the `Saved Services` page, with a service called `Migration1` selected and the `Run Service` command ready to be executed. From this page, services can also be edited as requirements change and deleted when they are not longer of use.

SFMS's ability to define and pre-store common storage management services eliminates much of the repetitive administrative work required to perform storage management operations that recur on a regular basis. Once a service is defined and saved, it can be executed as often as required, using the simple two-click invocation protocol illustrated in Figure 6-11. The facility for saving service definitions is also useful for common services that are invoked only occasionally. Pre-defining such services eliminates much of the potential for human error, by obviating the need for administrators to refresh their recollections of how to perform the service when it is required.

Finally, SFMS' ability to record arbitrary command sequences as custom services makes fast and accurate execution possible for almost any data center-specific management procedure.

Locating specific Storage Foundation objects

In a data center with thousands of managed objects, simply locating an object so management operations can be performed can be a non-trivial exercise. Storage Foundation Management Server includes a search facility that rapidly identifies specific objects or sets of objects. Figure 6-12 illustrates the SFMS search capability, using the example of a data center-wide search for VxFS file systems that occupy more than 100 megabytes of storage.

Figure 6-12 An SFMS object search (for VxFS file systems occupying more than 100 megabytes)

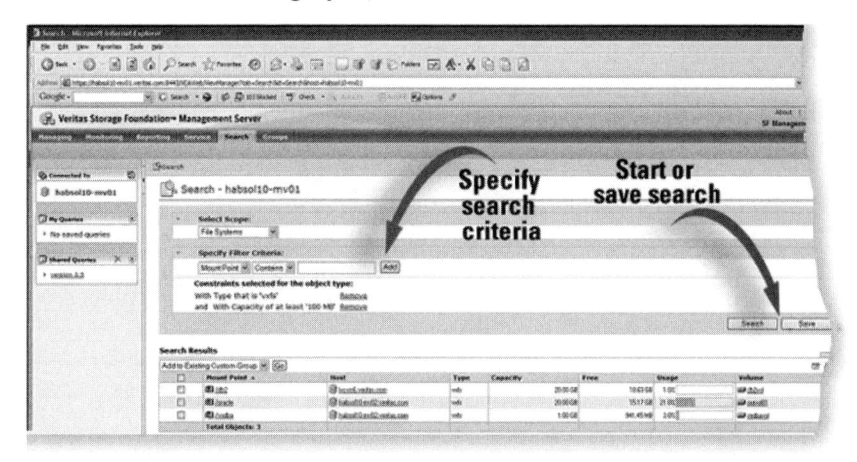

An administrator chooses an object type (disk, disk group, volume, file system, and so forth) and enters search criteria using the drop-downs in the upper left corner of the search page. Any number of search criteria can be entered. When a search has been completely formulated, it can be both saved for future reference and executed. Figure 6-12 shows the first few results of a search for VxFS file systems with a minimum size of 100 megabytes. As usual, the results are displayed in tabular form, and can be sorted on any column.

Summarizing the Storage Foundation Management Server

The Storage Foundation Management Server provides a central point from which administrators can gain an overall perspective of the storage-related resources in the data center, and carry out management operations on them. SFMS provides central facilities for monitoring, reporting, responding, and actively managing sets of Storage Foundation resources, extending the reach of a single administrator across the entire data center.

Administrators using SFMS can quickly identify and resolve storage problems within an overall data center context, with visibility to possible external ramifications of their decisions and actions. As with other Storage Foundation components, SFMS promotes improvements in the quality of storage service delivered by an IT organization to its clients, while at the same time reducing administrative cost by expanding the scope of observation and control that administrators can exercise.

Chapter 7

Using the Storage Foundation

This chapter includes the following topics:

Using advanced Storage Foundation facilities

The Veritas Storage Foundation provides comprehensive set of basic storage and data management services—host-based storage virtualization, scalable file management, management of storage network resources, and centralized management of all Storage Foundation resources. In addition to these, advanced features of the Storage Foundation simplify a number of the storage and data management problems that enterprise data centers face on a daily basis. This chapter describes five of these problems and shows how the Storage Foundation can be used to solve them quickly, reliably, and at lower cost:

- Migrating, or moving, data between different disk arrays, as for example, when an older array is replaced by a newer one

- Implementing a multi-tier storage architecture for one or more existing file systems
- Using bunker-style replication to provide data recovery at a distant location after a disaster with zero loss, while limiting the impact of replication on applications by replicating synchronously
- Moving data between unlike platforms, either as part of a change in computing strategy or for sharing data between applications that run on different platforms
- Reclaiming unneeded storage capacity from a file system, and consolidating it on separate disks that can be redeployed to other hosts

The sections that follow describe these five capabilities in more detail. They are representative of the ways in which standardizing on Storage Foundation throughout a data center can streamline storage administration, reduce capital and operating cost, and improve the quality of service delivered to clients.

Moving data between disk arrays

Data centers replace their disk arrays for any of several reasons. For example:

- Data growth requires greater online storage capacity
- New technology features motivate replacement of disk arrays by newer models
- Pricing considerations motivate change to a different storage vendor
- Disk arrays reach end of service life or end of lease

Whatever the reason for changing storage hardware, in almost all cases, the data stored on it must survive the change—data must be moved from old arrays to new ones. In today's typical data center, the storage capacity of a single disk array is shared by multiple application and database servers that connect to it via a storage network. Often, moving data from one array to another means application downtime, and moreover, requires coordination among all applications that share the source array.

The result of moving data is impact—impact on business operations due to application downtime and possible data loss, as well as impact on the IT budget, either because of administrative resource consumption or because of fees paid to storage consultants to take responsibility for moving data.

But the process of moving data between disk arrays is not inherently complex. It does, however, require that a number of individually executed steps be performed without error. The manual nature of the task and the number of error-free steps required create the potential for human error.

The process of moving data between disk arrays

When planning to move data from one disk array to another, an enterprise must first decide whether to restructure the data during the move. For example, if the new array has greater capacity than the old one, should larger LUNs be created on the new array? Should multi-volume file systems be used to consolidate existing file systems into a smaller number of name spaces to be managed by the Dynamic Storage Tiering facility (Multi-tier storage)?

Assuming for the moment that data is not restructured during the move, the process begins with the target array. Using array vendor-provided tools, a set of LUNs equivalent to those that exist on the source array must be defined, associated with the array's storage network ports (a process usually called binding), and masked and placed in storage network zones so that they are visible to the hosts that will require access to them, and to no others.

With the target disk array fully prepared, actually moving data to it from the source depends largely upon whether the source array is of the same type as the target array. Most disk array vendors provide replication tools that enable the movement of data between arrays of the same type. Generally, data can be copied from the source array to the target while it is in use by applications. When the copy is complete, applications must be adjusted to access their data from the LUNs on the target array rather than the source.

Moving data between disk arrays of different types is usually more problematic. Typically, application servers must discover the target array LUNs so that file systems can be created on them. Data is then copied from file systems on source arrays to equivalent file systems on the target arrays. To preserve the business consistency of data while it is copied, it must somehow be frozen, either by stopping applications that update it, or by making copies from snapshots, and logging updates that occur during the copy process so that they can be applied afterward.

Whether the move is homogeneous (between disk arrays of the same type) or heterogeneous (between disk arrays of different types), the process is sufficiently complex that enterprises tend to approach it as a major data center task, often spending substantial sums on contractors who manage the process from beginning to end and take responsibility for the results.

How Storage Foundation helps

Storage Foundation simplifies and reduces the operational impact of moving data between disk arrays in two important ways:

- It makes no distinction between moving data between homogeneous arrays and arrays of different types.

- It makes it possible to move data while it is in use, with no after-the-fact log playback required to catch up with updates made during the move.

After preparing a target array, as described earlier, and executing operating system device discovery processes on the affected hosts, a Storage Foundation administrator adds the newly-discovered target array LUNs to VxVM disk groups that contain the source volumes from which data will be copied. The administrator then adds an additional mirror (called a "plex" in VxVM terminology) to each source volume, using a target array LUN. The mirrors are allowed to synchronize, after which, the plexes made from source array LUNs are removed from the volume. When all of the source array's LUNs have been removed from service in this way, the source array can be retired or repurposed.

This procedure illustrates the two important advantages of using VxVM volumes as the basis for moving data:

- All of the VxVM operations, including adding mirrors to existing volumes, synchronizing the added mirrors' contents with those of the volume, and removing the source array-based plexes when synchronization is complete, are performed while data is being used by applications. No application downtime can be attributed to Storage Foundation operations. This greatly reduces the need for careful scheduling of inter-array data moves.
- VxVM can create a plex on any type of LUN and associate it with a volume whose plexes are made from LUNs presented by different types of disk arrays, possibly supplied by different vendors. Thus, with Storage Foundation, moving data between two arrays of the same type and moving data between arrays of different types are identical operations. This significantly reduces the barriers to moving data from one type of array to another.

This procedure involves only the VxVM component of Storage Foundation. VxVM can move volumes of data between arrays whether those volumes contain VxFS file systems, file systems of other types, or raw database data. Thus, the procedure can be applied equally well to all of a data center's data.

Other host-based volume managers, particularly those supplied by operating system vendors, have similar capabilities. With the Veritas Storage Foundation, however, the same operational procedures and management paradigms apply to all platforms that share access to an array. A single management paradigm means greater staff proficiency, more efficient execution, and fewer procedural errors during the migration process.

The rest of the story—Storage Foundation Management Server

This brief description of using Storage Foundation to move data between arrays is necessarily simplified. For example, realistically, an enterprise data center must use multiple paths to connect its storage to its application servers. When a new disk array is added to the network, the storage network path manager must be configured to handle the new LUNs as well.

But the greatest simplification in this description is that it omits the number of steps required to add a mirror to a VxVM volume, and the number of ancillary objects that must be created and coordinated. Thus, while the VxVM procedure simplifies the movement of data between arrays from the application users' point of view by eliminating downtime, it remains a significant administrative task.

For this reason, moving data between disk arrays is one of the pre-defined services that is incorporated into the Storage Foundation Management Server (SFMS). The SFMS web-based Service Builder includes a wizard-based volume movement service that guides an administrator through supplying the information required to move data from any number of VxVM volumes to volumes based on storage in a different array. Supplied with information about the source array, the volumes to be moved, and the target array, the Service Builder develops scripts that create and manipulate the VxVM objects necessary to accomplish the move. The scripts can be executed immediately, or execution can be deferred until a more convenient time. Because SFMS is web-based, an administrator can manage any Storage Foundation resources from any browser-equipped computer with a network connection to the SFMS server.

Thus, the Storage Foundation Management Server builds on the basic capabilities of VxVM that allow data to be moved from one disk array to another without disrupting applications by automating the details of the move, essentially reducing the administrative task to specification of the source and target for the move.

The net effect of Storage Foundation

The fundamental value propositions of the Storage Foundation when moving data between disk arrays are that it makes data movement independent of the type of array, and eliminates application downtime for the move itself (depending on the disk array and server platform, downtime may still be required for storage network configuration, device discovery, and so forth, but these causes of downtime are independent of the technique used to move data.

The SFMS Service Builder automates Storage Foundation-related steps in moving data, reducing administrative involvement to specification of the data sources and target arrays and scheduling a time for the move to begin. Automating data movement not only simplifies routine aspects of the administrator's job; it reduces the possibility of human error resulting in downtime, or worse, data loss.

Implementing a multi-tier storage architecture

The cost savings potential of a multi-tier storage deployment strategy is substantial. Over time, as lower-cost online storage is phased in, either in the form of arrays configured with low-cost disk drives, or simply by creating lower cost RAID5 configurations for storing infrequently-accessed data, a data center can save half or more of its online storage capital cost.

In most cases, the cost reduction carries little or no penalty. By limiting the contents of low-cost storage to non-critical or seldom-accessed data, a data center minimizes or eliminates any negative impact from the lower I/O performance of the low-cost devices on its overall operation.

Barriers to adopting multi-tier storage

But the prospect of implementing multi-tier storage can be daunting. Not only must administrators define what types of storage are most appropriate for the enterprise's online data, but they must also define application and operating policies that get data stored on the right devices in the first place, and move it to other devices as it ages and the notion of "right device" changes. Moreover, each time the location of a data set changes, administrators must adjust all applications and operating procedures that may use it to reflect its new location, or risk application failures and downtime.

How Storage Foundation helps

Storage Foundation multi-volume file systems and the Dynamic Storage Tiering (DST) facility combine to simplify the implementation of multi-tier online storage in two important ways:

- DST policy rules automatically place new data sets on the most appropriate type of virtual storage device, and cause existing data sets to be relocated to alternate devices when certain qualifying conditions, such as length of time since last access or modification, are met.
- A VxFS multi-volume file system distributes a single file system name space across multiple virtual volumes of different types. When DST relocates files from one storage tier to another, the files positions in the logical name space do not change, thus obviating any requirement for changes in applications or operating procedures.

Thus, the Storage Foundation eliminates the two major barriers to adopting multi-tier online storage and reaping the cost benefits that result from adoption—administrative complexity and the consequent risk of operational error.

Planning for multi-tier storage with Storage Foundation

Dynamic Storage Tiering automates the execution of administrator-defined policies for placing and relocating data within the confines of a multi-volume file system. DST eliminates the on-going administrative tasks implied by multiple storage tiers, but it does require advance planning to define policy rules that achieve enterprise objectives for data.

Planning to use DST requires three basic types of administrative decisions:

- The scope of data over which each DST instance should operate
- The types and capacities of storage devices required for each DST instance
- How data should be organized in directories or by user to facilitate the creation of policy rules

One of the benefits of DST is that it makes it possible to consolidate multiple file systems that may have been created mainly for the purpose of managing the locations of files back into a single name space. The first stage in planning to adopt DST is to decide which, if any, file systems will be consolidated into a single multi-volume one. Each set of file systems to be consolidated, typically representing the data for a single application or group of related applications, can be treated as an independent conversion project.

One file system, typically the largest one of the set to be consolidated, is chosen as a starting point. During the implementation, the volume that holds this file system is converted to a volume set, to which additional volumes are added to create storage tiers. The volume on which the starting point file system resides must be or must be made suitably robust to serve as the root metadata volume for the multi-volume file system that results from the conversion.

The second step in planning for DST is to determine the most appropriate types of storage devices to include in a multi-tier volume set and the initial capacity of each tier. This choice might be motivated by financial considerations, by the availability of existing hardware, by the typical I/O access patterns to which files are subjected, or, more likely, a combination of the three.

For example, if multi-tier storage is to be introduced by the purchase of a low-cost disk array, volumes based on the LUNs presented by the low-cost array will likely make up second-tier storage. Alternatively, if relatively inactive data is to be relegated to volumes based on RAID5 LUNs in an existing array, these must be configured using the array's own management tools. For transactional data, LUNs optimized for high I/O request rate should be prepared; for streaming data, high-bandwidth LUNs should be prepared.

In addition to the types of devices to be included among the storage tiers, an appropriate initial capacity for each tier should be chosen. The initial capacity need only be an estimate—at any time, additional capacity can be added to any tier of a file system's volume set, either in the form of additional volumes, or by expanding the capacity of a volume by increasing the storage resources available to it.

The third step in planning for DST is to determine how it should recognize files for the purpose of applying placement policy rules. Possible recognition criteria include the directory or subtree in which files reside, the owner's identifier, the identifier of the owning group, or a pattern according to which files are named. Typically, enterprises' files are already organized along these lines, but some adjustment may be necessary in order to keep file placement policies simple.

Some enterprises create multi-tier storage hierarchies for reasons other than cost. For example, databases of confidential business transactions or human resources records may be segregated from the general storage pool for security reasons. The department responsible for a set of data, the applications that process it, and the I/O patterns to which it is typically subjected are also sometimes used as criteria for creating different storage tiers on which different types of data are placed.

Controlling the placement of data objects within two or more tiers of storage can be useful to enterprises for several reasons:

- Different types of data have different I/O performance needs. Streams need high data transfer performance, but moderate I/O request rates are acceptable. Transactions need high I/O request rates but moderate data transfer performance.
- Applications that run concurrently may compete for I/O resources unless their data is placed on separate storage devices with separate access paths.
- Different data sets have different availability requirements. A typical enterprise can conduct business without its human resources system, but not without its point-of-sale or customer relationship management systems.
- Different data sets have different values to the enterprise. Loss of a day's business transactions is significant, but survivable. Losing annual closing figures might be catastrophic. Similarly, losing an entire day's work is significant to a video editor, but losing the finished product would be a much more serious setback for the editing company.
- Accounting, security, and regulatory compliance policies may require that certain storage devices be restricted to containing specific types of files.

As long as files with different values to the enterprise, I/O access patterns, policy requirements, and so forth, can be identified by their names, by the directories in which they reside, or by their owners, DST can place them properly within a multi-tier storage hierarchy.

Implementing multi-tier storage with Storage Foundation

Implementing DST for a particular set of data has five major steps:

- Creating the multi-volume file system that will house the data
- "Tagging" the file system's volumes to identify storage tiers or placement classes
- Creating and assigning a file placement policy
- Moving any data that is being consolidated to the target multi-volume file system
- Defining a policy enforcement schedule

Creating the multi-volume file system

VxFS multi-volume file systems are stored on VxVM volume set objects. From an administrative standpoint, a volume set is nothing more than a collection of VxVM volumes that have been identified as such. If a new multi-volume file system is being created, the volume set that will house it is created first, and the file system created on it using the VxFS `mkfs` command or the graphical equivalent provided by the Storage Foundation Management Server. If a single-volume file system is being converted to a multi-volume one, the file system's volume is converted to a one-volume volume set, and additional volumes are added to it.

The first volume in a volume set, known as volume 0, deserves special consideration. Unlike other volumes, volume 0 must be eligible to contain metadata (by default, it is the only volume in a volume set eligible to contain metadata). Because it contains the file system's most critical metadata structures, volume 0 should be the most failure-tolerant volume in a volume set. At a minimum, it should be mirrored. Consolidating several single-volume file systems into one multi-volume one effectively "puts more eggs in one basket." Consideration should be given to increasing the failure tolerance of volume 0 as more file systems are consolidated into one and the consequences of "losing" the volume become greater.

Other volumes are added to the volume based on requirements for I/O performance and data protection. For example:

- Mirrored volumes should be configured for high-value data. For an enterprise's most critical data, 3-mirror or 4-mirror volumes may be justified.
- For data that is normally streamed or accessed by transactional applications, striped volumes should be configured, with the number of "columns" dictated by performance requirements.

- RAID5 volumes can be configured for data of middling value that is not updated frequently with small write requests. LUNs presented by disk arrays populated with low-cost disks are normally suitable for data of this type.

Volume capacities may be approximate, because volumes can be expanded, and additional volumes can be added to a file system's volume set, but the average cost of a file system's storage is determined by the volumes that comprise it, so over-configuring the more expensive tiers leads to a higher-than-necessary aggregate storage cost.

Tagging the volumes

From the viewpoint of DST, a storage tier is one or more of the volumes in a file system's volume set that have a common file placement policy tag value. Thus, which volumes comprise a storage tier for a given file system is completely at the discretion of the administrator. Because VxFS distributes files approximately equally across the volumes comprising a tier, however, the best practice is to create tiers that consist of identical volumes, or at a minimum, volumes of nearly identical failure tolerance and performance.

If storage tiers are defined based on volume I/O performance and failure tolerance properties, two or three tiers should suffice in most cases. If files are segregated for other reasons, such as regulatory compliance, additional tiers may be required. Normally, a single volume in each tier is sufficient at the outset. As more data is acquired, additional volumes can be added to a tier. For file systems that grow and shrink frequently by the addition and removal of files, however, it may be desirable to create storage tiers with multiple volumes so that volumes can be removed and redeployed elsewhere when necessary.

Defining and assigning the file placement policy

File locations in a multi-volume file system are controlled by the active file placement policy assigned to it. Administrators create XML file placement policy documents using either text editors or, for certain common types of policies, graphical wizards supplied with VxFS and with the Storage Foundation Management Server.

A file placement policy consists of rules, each of which applies to a selected set of files designated by name, owner, or directory. Each rule specifies the storage tier, or placement class, on which VxFS is to create selected files, and one or more qualifying conditions under which files should be moved to other storage tiers.

File placement policy rules are specified in terms of storage tiers rather than specific volumes. This has two important advantages:

- Because the volume tags that define storage tiers need not be unique in a system, any number of file systems can use the same tag values. O single file placement policy can be applied to any file system whose volumes are tagged with the storage tier names specified in the policy.
- A storage tier can easily be expanded or shrunk by the addition or removal of volumes that belong to the tier. No modification of the active policy is required; VxFS simply applies it to whatever volumes are part of the file system's volume set.

Thus, a data center with many similar servers, for example database or web servers, can use the Storage Foundation Management Server to define a single file placement policy which it can assign to all of them. Not only does this reduce administrative workload, it promotes storage management standardization across the data center, even across platforms of different types.

VxFS file placement policies specify rules for initial file placement and relocation. Most files are accessed frequently when they are first created, so policy rules should typically specify creation on a high-performance storage tier.

As files age, they tend to become inactive. Because they are highly likely to be backed up, inactive files can be relocated to lower-cost storage devices that may provide lower I/O performance and be less failure tolerant with little or no impact on overall data center performance. Any of the access age, modification age, I/O temperature, and access temperature qualifiers can be specified as relocation criteria in placement policy rules.

VxFS can automatically relocate files from higher storage tiers to lower ones as well as the reverse. For downward relocation, lower bounds on access age and modification age, or upper bounds on I/O temperature and access temperature are normally specified. For example, selected files that are on top-tier storage may be relocated downward if access age is greater than 30 days, or alternatively, if I/O temperature drops below 10. For upward relocation, the reverse is specified—for example, a file on lower-tier storage may be relocated to upper-tier storage if access age drops below 10 days, or if I/O temperature rises above 7.

Placement policy rules can also be used to segregate designated files from the general storage pool, for example, for fiscal or regulatory compliance reasons. Segregation is accomplished by tagging one or more volumes in the file system's volume set uniquely, and writing a placement policy rule specifying that the files to be segregated should be created on the uniquely tagged volume(s) and not relocated.

The file placement behavior of VxFS is sensitive to the order in which policy rules are specified. The first rule in a policy that specifies a given file is the only rule that VxFS uses to place or relocate that file. Thus, administrators should exercise care when creating file placement policies. In general, more specific rules should precede more general ones in a policy document.

Moving data into and within the multi-volume file system

If a Dynamic Storage Tiering implementation includes consolidation of two or more file systems, the final implementation step is to copy files into the consolidated multi-volume file system before deleting the file systems from which it came and redeploying the storage they occupy. Whether the consolidated file system is a newly-created one, or one of the original file systems that has been made into a multi-volume one, the copying files into it effectively creates new files. Newly-created files are placed according to initial placement rules, not according to recent activity against the source files from which they were copied.

If the consolidated file system's policy is age-oriented, creating files on top-tier storage and relocating them to lower storage tiers if they are inactive for a period of time, that period must elapse before VxFS can discover that files are inactive and relocate them.

If policy rules specify "safety valves"—secondary storage tiers to be used if the primary one is full, the consequence of copying large numbers of files into a consolidated file system is minor. VxFS will perform "extra" relocations as it discovers over time that certain files are actually inactive. If, however, no secondary tiers are specified, file copy operations that populate the consolidated file system may fail.

For this reason, administrators who are consolidating files from several file systems into a single multi-volume for use with the DST facility should consider creating and assigning temporary policies during initial population of the consolidated file system. In general, these temporary policies would create designated files on lower storage tiers. For example, if files from a file system containing historical data are copied into the `/history` path of the consolidated file system, a temporary policy rule might specify that files in the `/history` directory and all of its subdirectories be created on second-tier storage.

Such a temporary policy has the effect of placing most files appropriately as they are added to the consolidated file system. It is necessary because VxFS requires historical information about files to make relocation decisions, and such historical information is not available when files are newly added to a file system. When initial population of a consolidated file system is complete, the temporary policy should be replaced by assigning a permanent one that accurately reflects the data center's long-term intent.

Defining a file placement policy enforcement schedule

VxFS enforces file placement policies on administrative command. Policy enforcement is typically done by scheduling `cron` jobs at regular intervals (for example, daily), at times when production activity is expected to be low. During policy enforcement, VxFS relocates each qualifying (for example, inactive) file to a destination placement class if space is available. If a destination placement class is full, no relocation occurs.

The net effect of Storage Foundation

The VxFS Dynamic Storage Tiering (DST) facility makes it possible to actually reap the cost, performance, and security benefits of multi-tier storage without incurring an offsetting administrative burden on the data center. DST has two parts: multi-volume file systems and automatic policy-based placement of files within a file system's storage.

Bunker replication

Increasingly, enterprises are recognizing that certain digital data sets are critical to their operation, and, in extreme cases, to their survival. With the natural and other disasters that have occurred in recent years in mind, they have become acutely conscious of the need to make critical data proof against disasters that may incapacitate their data centers. Most industries that society deems critical, like defense, finance, health care, and so forth, are required by law or other regulation to protect their digital records against destruction due to any conceivable threat.

Parameters of disaster recovery plans

Disaster recovery plans for preserving data and making it accessible after disasters are becoming commonplace among large enterprises, and can be found in some smaller enterprises as well. Disaster recovery plans vary widely, but are universally driven by two key parameters:

- Recovery time objective, or the time between the disaster and the restoration of access to critical data and applications
- Recovery point objective, or the point in time represented by critical data at the moment of recovery

Disaster recovery times are a function of many variables, including the speed of recognition and response to the disaster, the readiness of the recovery facilities, both IT and environmental, the availability of staff to operate the recovery location, the impact of the disaster on the physical environment, and so forth. Many of these factors are beyond the control of the enterprise.

Recovery points are primarily a function of the techniques used to preserve data against destruction. In the past, point-in-time backup copies of critical data on tapes stored at a distance from the data center have been the primary recovery mechanism. Transporting a backup tape set (which may represent a point in time days or weeks prior to the disaster) to the recovery site and restoring it can result in recovery points that are literally weeks prior to the disaster. Today, this is inadequate for most enterprises. For their truly critical data, enterprises typically adopt some form of network-based replication that transmits updates to critical data to a remote location, where they are applied to a copy of the production data, keeping it up to date, or nearly so.

Properties of data replication solutions

Online data can be replicated at several levels. Tools are available for replicating disk array LUNs, VxVM volumes, files, and databases. Each level is unique in terms of what updates are copied, when copying occurs, and how updates are applied to a copy of production data at the recovery location. The most prevalent form of replication is the LUN or virtual volume, possibly because replicating virtual devices replicates everything on the devices, including both database tables and indexes and any ancillary files, software images, scripts, and so forth, that might be required to operate an application. When virtual devices are replicated, production data updates, patches to applications, modifications to operating scripts, and so forth, are all copied to the recovery location in real or nearly real time. As long as the correct devices are replicated, there is no concern about critical control files, software libraries and so forth not being available at the recovery location when they are needed.

As with most aspects of disaster recovery, the major issue with data replication is cost. The biggest capital cost of IT disaster recovery is the recovery site—the premises, equipment, and connectivity required to resume an enterprise's key applications after a disaster. Most large enterprises wish to place their recovery data centers far (hundreds or even thousands of miles) from their production data center, so that the probability of a disaster affecting both is vanishingly remote.

But locating a recovery data center hundreds of miles from the production one creates a dilemma. On the one hand, up-to-date data at a recovery location is more valuable than out-of date data. For high-value applications, such as commercial funds transfer, it may even be crucial. But keeping remote data completely up-to-date (synchronized) means that updates to both production and remote data must be complete before an application thread can proceed. In an enterprise-scale transaction processing system that may experience hundreds of updates per second, keeping remote data up-to-date requires extremely high (expensive) network bandwidth. Moreover, for recovery centers that are hundreds or thousands of miles from production data center, completely up-to-date data may simply be impossible because the time required to propagate updates through a long-distance network with complex and varying topology increases application response time intolerably.

Conventional solutions

Figure 7-1 illustrates the conventional mechanism for maintaining an up-to-date replica of critical production data for disaster recovery, sometimes referred to as a bunker strategy. A physically secure bunker site is established far enough from the production data center that it is unlikely to be affected by a disaster at the production center, but near enough so that production data can be replicated synchronously. The bunker site requires only basic processing resources, but sufficient mirrored storage to replicate the entire production data set.

Figure 7-1 Conventional disaster recovery data replication scenario

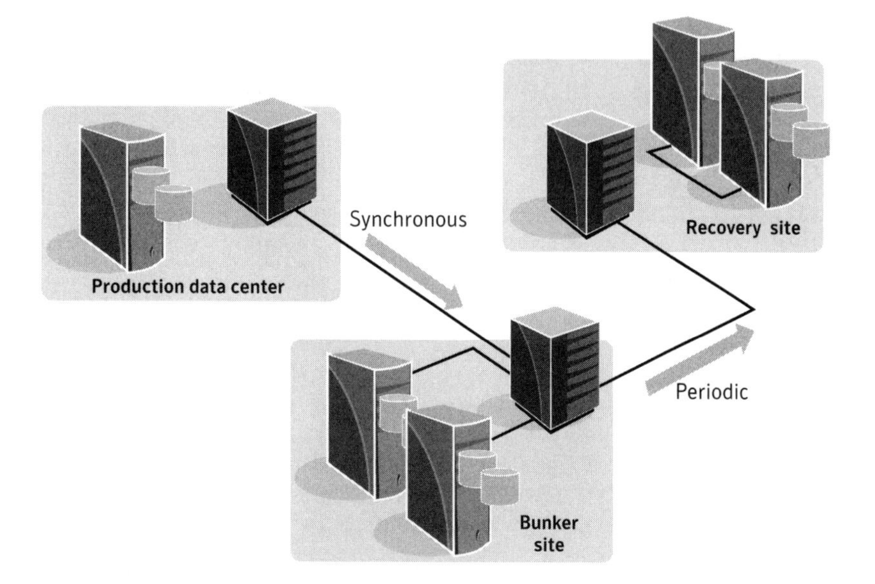

In addition to the bunker site, a fully-equipped recovery center is established at a greater distance from the production center. The distance is such that the recovery center offers protection against almost any conceivable disaster, but is too great for synchronous replication of production data to be practical.

With this configuration, data is replicated synchronously to mirrored storage devices at the bunker site, so there is always an up-to-date copy available outside the production data center. Periodically, the mirrors at the bunker site are split, effectively creating a snapshot of production data. The snapshot is replicated asynchronously to storage devices the recovery center, and when replication is complete, the mirrors at the bunker site are resynchronized with the on-going synchronous replica of the production data.

In this scenario, the recovery site is also equipped with two sets of storage devices, for two complete copies of production data. Data is replicated alternately to each set of devices. When replication is complete, the older devices may be synchronized with the newer ones. Thus, no matter when in the replication cycle a disaster occurs, the recovery site has a complete recent snapshot of production data. The age of the replica, which is determined by the frequency of periodic replication from the bunker site, is the recovery point—the amount of time by which data is out-of-date when recovery commences.

While this procedure provides good guarantees against data loss due to physical disaster, it has some shortcomings:

- It requires a large investment in storage. In addition to storage for the actual production data, sufficient storage for two copies of production data at each of the bunker and recovery sites is required—a total of five times the storage required to contain production data. Disk array-based solutions require that all replicated storage be homogeneous—if premium disk arrays are used for production data, all replicas must be on premium arrays as well.
- It is bandwidth-intensive. Replicating data from bunker site to recovery site should be frequent, to keep recovery point objectives low, but this effectively means that the link between the two sites is in use constantly. If inadequate bandwidth between the bunker and recovery sites is configured, periodic replication will be slow, and recovered data will be older relative to the moment of disaster.
- The resulting replica at the recovery site is inherently out-of-date. Each time data is replicated from the bunker site to the recovery site, it is frozen in time at the start of replication. The replica at the recovery site cannot be used until it is complete. Therefore, it is out of date by at least the time required to replicate the entire data set.

Thus, while fundamentally effective, the conventional procedure is expensive in terms of storage and network resources consumed, and inherently limited in the recovery points it can produce.

How Storage Foundation helps

With Version 5, the Veritas Volume Replicator (VVR) optional component of the Storage Foundation simplifies bunker replication significantly. VVR is a host-based facility for replicating arbitrary sets of VxVM volumes to as many as 32 target locations. VVR replicates production data updates either synchronously or asynchronously to each replication target. Because VVR replicates the contents of VxVM virtual volumes, there is no requirement that source and target hardware be the same. Thus, low-cost storage can be employed as replication targets for situations in which any use of the replica as production data is likely to be short-lived.

VVR is log-based. Every application update to production data is written to a Storage Replication Log (SRL) before being transmitted to replication targets. Data remains in the SRL until all replication targets have acknowledged receiving it. Application write requests do not complete until all targets for which replication is synchronous have acknowledged receipt of the updated data. If all replicas are asynchronous, application write requests complete as soon as data has been written to the SRL. A single set of source volumes, called a replication volume group (RVG), may contain both synchronous and asynchronous targets.

Within a replication volume group, write order fidelity is preserved. Updates to all volumes in a group are applied in the same order in which applications update the source volumes. Thus, any file system or database crash recovery mechanisms that rely on the order in which data is written can be applied to the volumes in an RVG just as they would be applied to the production data in the event of a system crash.

A new capability of Version 5 of the Storage Foundation is VVR's ability to effectively make a RVG's storage replication log part of the RVG, and replicate it. This capability leads to a significant simplification of bunker-style replication for disaster recovery, which is illustrated in Figure 7-2.

Figure 7-2 Storage Foundation disaster recovery data replication scenario

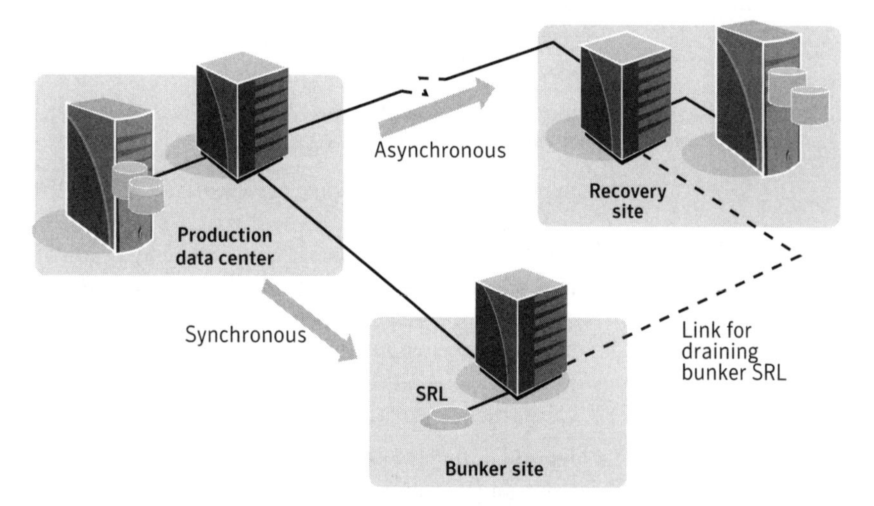

As Figure 7-2 suggests, VVR replicates production data asynchronously directly to the recovery site, while it replicates SRL contents (but not production data) synchronously to the Bunker site. Since SRLs are sized based on a combination of the expected rate of updates to production and the expected duration of any brief network outages, they are typically small compared to the size of the production data set. Thus, the storage requirement at the bunker site is significantly less than with the conventional solution illustrated in Figure 7-1.

With asynchronous replication, the state data at a target site can fall behind that of the production data if, for example, there is a momentary network overload or an interval of especially heavy production data update activity. If either of these occurs, VVR simply allows the SRL to fill, in the expectation that it will drain when the momentary overload is past. This principle can be extended to accommodate occasional brief network outages—VVR can allow the SRL to fill with production data updates while the network is out of service, and drain it to the replication target site when network connectivity is restored. Administrators can tune the amount by which asynchronous replication can fall behind production data updates.

With VVR bunker replication, production data is replicated asynchronously to the recovery site, and can therefore be out of date by a few seconds or minutes when a disaster occurs. But because replication of the SRL to the bunker site is synchronous, it is in lockstep with production data. If a disaster occurs at the production center, the Veritas Cluster Server Global Cluster Option (VXS GCO) coordinates the VVR instances at the production, bunker, and recovery sites. The VVR instance at the bunker site effectively becomes the replication source. It drains the SRL to the VVR instance at recovery site, which applies updates to its replica. When the SRL has been drained completely, the data image at the recovery site represents the state of the production data at the moment of the disaster. In effect, a recovery point of zero, that is, recovery of production data to its state at the moment of disaster, is achieved.

A quick comparison of Figure 7-1 with Figure 7-2 makes clear the advantages of the VVR bunker replication solution:

- Significantly lower storage requirements. With VVR, the production and recovery sites require sufficient virtual storage to contain the production data set. The storage at either or both sites may be mirrored to meet business requirements, but additional copies are not required by VVR. At the bunker site, all that is required is sufficient storage for the SRL, which it typically a small fraction of the production data set size. Moreover, there is no requirement that storage at all sites be of the same type. Low-cost or repurposed storage can be deployed at the bunker and recovery sites if business needs dictate that.
- Significantly lower bandwidth requirements. With VVR, adequate bandwidth between production and recovery sites to keep pace with the steady-state rate

of updates to production data is required. VVR handles momentary overloads by allowing the SRL to fill. Adequate short-distance bandwidth between production and bunker sites to keep pace with SRL activity is also required. There is no requirement for massive bandwidth between bunker and recovery sites, because the only action between the two is draining of the SRL if a disaster occurs.

- Zero recovery point objective. With VVR, data at the recovery site is up-to-date at the time of a disaster, unless the disaster occurs during a period of network overload or outage. If recovery site data is out-of-date, VVR at the bunker site continues to play the SRL to the recovery site until it is drained and the data at the recovery site is up-to-date. The replica of data at the recovery site can be updated to the state of production data at the moment of disaster.

Thus, VVR bunker replication can sharply reduce the cost of bunker-style replication, and at the same time, provide a significantly improved quality of service in terms of a so-called zero recovery point.

The net effect of Storage Foundation

The Storage Foundation VVR option eliminates most of the need for extra storage in bunker-style disaster recovery situations, while at the same time, providing the powerful advantage of data recoverability to the moment of disaster. It can enable disaster recoverability for applications and large data sets for which conventional bunker techniques are too expensive or insufficiently timely.

Moving data between unlike platforms

As digital data processing increasingly pervades the fields of business, government, and education, and as data centers strive to reduce cost and increase flexibility by deploying more and more servers, moving data between servers is becoming an almost daily task in information technology organizations. Indeed, for an enterprise with a thousand servers, a service lifetime of five years means that a server is replaced approximately every second day. In almost all cases, applications and, more importantly, data, must survive server retirement. Almost daily, data must be moved from older servers to newer ones.

With storage networks, moving data from an old server to a new one of the same type should be simple enough. Administrators remove the older server from the data's network zone, and add the replacement server to the zone. The new server is booted and discovers the storage devices containing the data. Administrators mount the file systems, and the move is complete.

Barriers to changing platforms

The flaw in this argument is that it only works if the old and new servers are similar platforms—both Solaris/SPARC or both HP-UX/PA-RISC systems, for example. To move data between platforms of different types requires copying it from the format of one to the format of the other, usually by network file transfer protocol (FTP) or by backup to a neutral tape format and restore to file systems on the new server platform. Whichever of these techniques is used to move data between unlike platforms, administrative labor and application downtime are the result. FTP transfers are generally faster and easier to administer than backup and restore, but have the disadvantages of requiring extra storage for the duration of the copy, and of consuming large amounts of network bandwidth. The net effect is that the need to move data between platforms makes IT organizations inflexible. Enterprises may forego server cost or technology improvements if they imply a change in platform, and the consequent need to transform application data from one platform's format to that of another.

The unlike online data formats used by different UNIX and Linux operating systems limit data center flexibility in other ways as well. For example, low-cost Linux servers would be cost-effective for off-host backup of snapshots of production data that is processed by enterprise UNIX systems. But the resources and time required to transform Solaris or AIX data for use by Linux usually preclude this option. Similarly, auxiliary applications like data mining on alternate platforms, as well as the testing of new software or database formats on alternate platforms are usually precluded by the inability of one platform to process snapshots of data in the format used by another.

The root of the problem

The fundamental reason for the need to transform data for use on alternate platforms is that each platform has its own format for host-based virtual storage devices and file system data and metadata. The reasons for this are largely historical. Most of the server platforms in use today were developed during an era when data processing was largely homogeneous—enterprises tended to standardize on a single vendor product line for entire classes of applications for relatively long periods of time. More recently, however, two factors have combined to change this dynamic:

- The IT industry has evolved from a vertically integrated to a horizontally integrated one. Today, enterprises are much more likely to standardize on preferred vendors and product lines each layer in the information technology stack—for storage, servers, network components, operating systems, database management systems, infrastructure software, and applications.

- The pace of technology change has accelerated significantly, particularly in storage and servers. Today, it is not uncommon for enterprises to replace servers and disk arrays not because they have exceeded their useful lifetimes, but because it is no longer cost-effective to own and maintain them, given newer technology that is available. Useful lifetimes for data center equipment have moved from five years to three years, and in some cases, even less.

But as the pace of change accelerates, the legacy of unique online data formats for every platform remains, limiting flexibility and stifling creative use of online information assets.

How Storage Foundation helps

Current shipping versions of the Storage Foundation eliminate the entire problem of transforming data for use on different enterprise UNIX platforms. The solution begins with the VxVX Cross-platform Data Sharing (CDS) disk format that makes it possible to transfer control of volumes intact between any two supported UNIX or Linux platforms. CDS is the default format for newly created VxVM disk groups, and older groups can be upgraded to it by administrative action. Volumes created on disks in CDS format are known as Portable Data Containers (PDCs).

Similarly, the Version 6 VxFS file system layout is identical for all supported enterprise UNIX platforms (except for some small limitations of the platforms themselves, such as maximum file name lengths and directory tree depths). This allows VxFS file systems on VxVM volumes to be transferred intact between unlike UNIX platforms simply by transferring control of the disks they occupy.

Transferring file systems between enterprise UNIX and Linux systems is slightly more complicated because of the underlying processor architectures of the two. File system metadata contains many multi-byte integers, which are stored and interpreted differently by the big-endian computers typical of enterprise UNIX systems than they are by the little-endian systems that run Linux. VxFS provides a utility program that converts the metadata in an unmounted file system between the two formats. If a file system is unmounted and this utility runs against it, it can be moved from a UNIX to a Linux system or the reverse by transferring control of the disks that contain its volumes.

The ability to transfer entire file systems between unlike hosts quickly and with little resource impact is particularly powerful when combined with snapshots. A volume-level snapshot of a file system can be transferred from, for example, an AIX host to a Solaris host for backup or mining of the data in it simply by splitting the disks that comprise its volumes from their disk group, deporting them, importing them on the Solaris host and starting the volumes. The file system on the volumes can be mounted and used directly.

Using Storage Foundation to move data between unlike platforms

To use Storage Foundation facilities to move data between two different platforms, the two platforms must be physically connected to the same storage network. Transferring control of the data includes the following steps:

- The file system containing the data to be moved (which may be a multi-volume file system) is unmounted from its host system.
- If the source and destination systems run on processors with different integer addressing ("endianness"), a VxFS utility program is run against the volume(s) containing the unmounted file system to convert file system metadata. If source and target systems use the same integer formats, this step is not required.
- The disks containing the volume(s) containing the file system to be moved are split from their disk group and deported from the source system. If the volumes are actually represent a snapshot of production data that remains on the source host, the snapshot's cache volume must be deported along with the snapshot itself.
- Storage network zones and disk array LUN masks are adjusted as necessary so that the destination can access the disks containing the data. If installation policy requires it, additional adjustment may be performed to ensure that the source system can no longer access the disks being moved.
- The disks containing the deported volume(s) are imported on the destination system, the volumes they contain are started, and the file systems on them are mounted. At this point, data can be used by auxiliary applications on the destination system. If the data was moved permanently, as for example, from a server being retired to its replacement, the data is permanently associated with the replacement server.
- If the auxiliary application is a periodic one, for example, weekly backup or analysis, the volumes (including the cache volume) are deported from the destination system when the application completes. The volumes are then imported on the source system, added back into their original disk group, where VxVM uses FastResync™ to resynchronize them with the production file system, so that the process can be repeated when it is time for the next auxiliary processing cycle.

Moving data between two unlike platforms running Storage Foundation requires that the disks to be moved not contain any VxVM objects that cannot be removed from the source system. The best practice is to construct volumes that will contain data that may be moved among hosts using disks or LUNs that are dedicated to that one purpose.

The net effect of Storage Foundation

Network file copying may be adequate for moving modest amounts of data from one platform to another unlike platform. But when the data sets in question consist of multiple terabytes copying data at about three hours per terabyte can result in substantial downtime. If source and destination systems both run the Storage Foundation, with CDS volumes and Version 6 VxFS file system layouts, the need for copying data can be obviated by transferring control of the disks containing the data from the source system to the destination one, a task usually accomplished in at most a few minutes.

For permanent server replacements, Storage Foundation can reduce the downtime required to migrate applications and data from the old server to the new one significantly. One important consequence of this is the reduction of a significant barrier to changing system architectures—applications must still be ported or versions designed for the new platform used, but data can be made available to the new system whenever the time is ripe, even if the new server has a different integer data architecture ("endianness").

By cutting the time to move large data sets between unlike platforms from hours to minutes and eliminating network traffic, Storage Foundation can actually enable auxiliary applications that might not otherwise be viable. Particularly when the data moved is a set of coordinated VxVM volume snapshots, Storage Foundation makes it possible to analyze up-to-the-minute images of production data for business advantage.

Storage capacity reclamation

An important value proposition often cited for storage networks is the ability to redeploy storage resources from systems that no longer require them to systems that need additional storage. In principle, the proposition is valid, but the benefit may be more difficult to achieve than it would seem because the storage to be reclaimed is likely to be occupied by data. This is especially true of top-tier storage that has been freed by implementing a second storage tier and using the Dynamic Storage Tiering facility to relocate data to the second tier. The value proposition of DST is that it frees top-tier storage for use elsewhere, but the top-tier storage is occupied by the VxVM volume that originally contained the entire file system, and still contains the file system's metadata.

For example, a file system's top-tier storage may be a one terabyte striped mirrored volume that occupies ten 200 gigabyte disks, 90% of whose capacity has been freed by installing a low-cost second storage tier and using DST to relocate data to it. In principle, eight of the top-tier disks could be redeployed, but the 100 gigabytes of data that remain on top-tier storage are striped across all ten pairs of mirrored disks. Similar scenarios would arise with data striped across disk array LUNs.

The conventional solution

The conventional mechanism for reclaiming storage in a network is to create a LUN or volume of the new required size, 200 gigabytes in this example (allowing for 100% future growth of top-tier data), copy the data to it, and reclaim the entire LUN or volume that had previously been occupied by the data. This procedure carries an obvious cost in downtime and bandwidth, and in addition, may result in a need to changes in applications or scripts. Because both the new device and the device to be reclaimed must be present on the system simultaneously during the copy, both must occupy unique storage network addresses. When the data has been copied and the reclaimed device removed from the system, there must be some adjustment, either in how applications and scripts address the new device, or in the network address of the new device, so that the resized data is visible to the applications that need it. Either technique results in more downtime and more risk of error.

How Storage Foundation helps

Reclamation of storage capacity for redeployment is a particularly good example of how the close integration between Storage Foundation components simplifies data center administration. With two simple operations, an administrator can reduce the size of a VxFS file system, reclaim storage capacity from the volume it occupies, and consolidate the remaining volume capacity so that the reclaimed storage is on separate devices and can be redeployed elsewhere. Figure 7-3 shows how the Storage Foundation can reclaim storage capacity from a VxFS file system that occupies a striped volume spread over five disks.

Figure 7-3 Using Storage Foundation to reclaim storage capacity

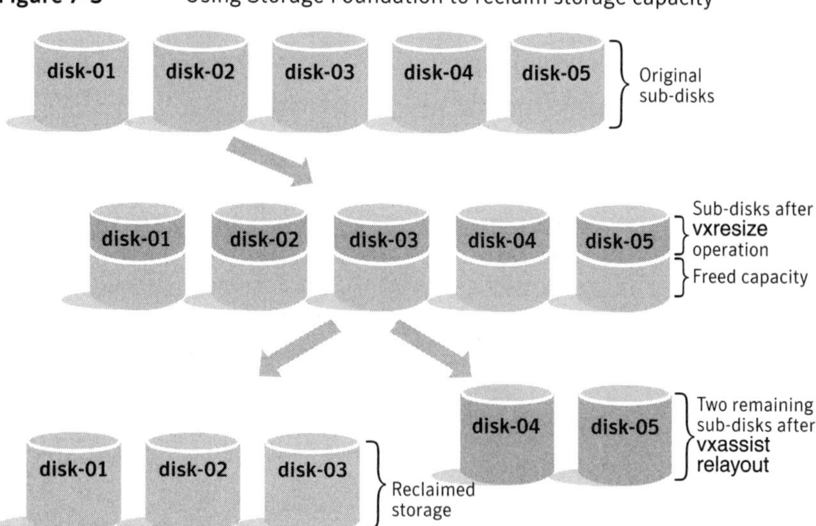

VxVM volumes are made up from blocks of disk storage capacity that are called sub-disks. The top row of Figure 7-3 represents a striped volume that occupies the entire capacity of five disks. The entire capacity of the volume is occupied by a VxFS file system.

The `vxresize` administrative command can shrink (or grow) the capacity of a VxFS file system by any specified amount. Integral to the command's execution is a corresponding shrinkage of the underlying VxVM volume. VxVM attempts to shrink all subdisks that comprise a volume equally. As Figure 7-3 illustrates, this frees some, but not all of the capacity of all of the disks that comprise the volume.

In this state, the options for redeploying storage are limited. One or more new volumes can be created from the freed capacity, but because the disks that contain the freed capacity must remain accessible to the original host (because they contain the resized original volume), the freed capacity cannot be logically disconnected from the original host and deployed elsewhere.

A second operation called `vxassist relayout` is required to consolidate the space occupied by the resized volume, also consolidating the freed capacity in the process. In the example, the resized volume is consolidated into two columns (sub-disks), and in the process, the entire capacity of the other three disks is freed for redeployment on the same host (or others, because there is no longer a need to keep the freed disks in the same disk group or logically connected to the host).

The file system resize-volume relayout sequence can all be executed while the file system is online and being accessed by production applications, although the background I/O load that results from the volume relayout may have some impact on production application performance.

The net effect of Storage Foundation

Storage Foundation's ability to reduce the size of a file system that is in use, automatically reduce the size of the underlying volume, and consolidate the freed storage capacity for redeployment on other hosts simplifies and reduces the resources required for and the downtime implied by reclamation of storage capacity for deployment elsewhere in the data center. Storage Foundation makes the promise of storage flexibility that is enabled by storage networks into a practical reality. Because there is little impact on production applications from the two-step Storage Foundation reclamation operation, data centers may be inclined to reclaim and redeploy online storage more aggressively, thus improving utilization, reducing cost, and providing better quality of service to applications.

Summarizing Storage Foundation advanced capabilities

The five examples presented in this chapter are representative of how Storage Foundation simplifies storage administration, particularly for large, complex data centers in which multiple server platforms are deployed. Other examples could be cited, including the use of space-saving snapshots to move data between hosts for auxiliary processing, automation of storage provisioning so that enterprise intent for data is preserved when volumes and file systems are expanded, copying data between devices with minimal impact on production applications using the data, and so forth. A data center with multiple computing platforms and dozens of servers is usually well-served by a detailed study of the capabilities of Symantec's Storage Foundation with an eye toward how Storage Foundation could be used to improve its management of its online storage assets.

Chapter 8

Making standardization happen

This chapter includes the following topics:

- The case for standardizing storage management
- Setting goals for standardization
- The two faces of storage management standardization
- Implementing storage management standardization
- From here to standardization
- Summary: standardizing on the Storage Foundation

The case for standardizing storage management

Software standardization is the primary tool available to enterprises for bringing the cost of managing their online storage under control. The preceding chapters make the case that the Veritas Storage Foundation by Symantec has the necessary attributes to be the standard tool set for managing online storage in enterprise data centers, including:

- Complete capabilities, both basic and advanced, for "one-stop shopping" for storage management functionality
- Complete system and storage platform support so that administrative skills become universally applicable throughout the data center
- Integration with the rest of the application-storage stack for consolidation of storage management operations

- Integration with storage applications like backup managers, database management systems, and vendor-supplied low-level management tools for end-to-end storage management

While the proposition is attractive, to a data center manager or CIO looking at an existing installation, the path to achieving standardization may appear daunting. This chapter describes a set of steps for moving from an ad hoc storage management environment to an environment more aligned with the well-known storage utility concept—the efficient delivery of standardized services, primarily through the use of standardized tools.

Setting goals for standardization

An old adage states that "if you don't know where you're going, you may wind up somewhere else." This is as true for storage management standardization as for any other organized activity. A plan to standardize storage management should begin with realistic goal-setting to estimate the potential benefits.

Standardizing storage management tools, techniques, and practices provides three types of benefits:

- Lower operating costs, achieved by increasing the efficiency of administrative personnel, both through automation and more focused expertise
- Capital cost savings, achieved by reducing the number of software licenses and maintenance agreements as well as by reducing the on-going cost of storage hardware
- Improved quality of service, achieved by improving storage utilization, I/O performance, recoverability from user errors, failure tolerance, and disaster recoverability

A goal is necessarily reached from a starting point. It is often the case that IT organizations simply do not have comprehensive knowledge of what storage exists in their data centers, how well it is utilized, and what tools are being used to manage it. Before the potential benefits of standardizing storage management throughout the data center can be determined, an IT organization must understand the current situation, both in terms of operating and capital cost and in terms of desirable or required services that aren't being delivered. The sections that follow give some guidelines for determining a data center's current storage management situation as a prelude to determining the benefits that might reasonably be expected from standardization.

Capital cost savings potential

One of the first steps in determining a data center's current cost of storage management is to take an inventory of major hardware and software components and major data sets as suggested by the example in Table 8-1.

Table 8-1 Storage inventory

Item	Components and properties included in inventory
Storage hardware	Disk arrays and directly-attached disks. Should include vendors, models, hardware and firmware revision levels, number and types of disk drives, controller ports, current connections, and so forth
Storage network	Switches, directors, and other storage network hardware. Should include models, hardware and firmware revision levels, number and type of ports, current connections, and so forth
Virtualization	Types and implementations of virtual storage. Should include mirrored, RAID, striped, replicated, and other forms of virtual storage, as well as virtualization tools used (host-based, network-based, disk array-based), and the host and storage platforms on which they operate
Advanced functions	Advanced storage functions such as snapshots, replication, storage network path management; types of implementation (host-based, network-based, disk array-based), and the host and storage platforms on which they operate
Management tools	Number of storage management tools in use, functions for which they are used, and host and storage platforms on which they operate
Data sets	Number, size, and criticality of major file systems and databases in the data center. How many copies of data sets are maintained, their currency, and the reasons maintaining them
Storage clients	Application and database servers that use storage. Should include databases, file systems used by the applications, as well as other storage-related application characteristics

Such an inventory, combined with other preparatory steps, can help an enterprise determine a variety of useful information about potential benefits of storage management standardization:

- Whether there are savings to be realized by increasing the utilization of existing storage and storage network capacity
- Whether savings could be realized by employing a multi-tier storage strategy for online data
- Whether the business value of different data sets to the enterprise is commensurate with the quality of service delivered by the storage configurations that contain them

The results of a storage and data inventory should clarify the potential capital savings from standardizing storage management. For example:

- If space-saving snapshots can supplant entire copies of large or slowly-changing data sets for the purpose of protecting against data corruption, less storage hardware may be required at any point in time.
- If non-critical or seldom-accessed data sets can be moved to low-cost storage hardware, or protected by RAID5 rather than by mirroring, average cost per usable byte of storage can be reduced.
- If data sets can be moved between different platforms for serial reuse, the cost of storage and network bandwidth for creating and maintaining intermediate or redundant copies of data sets can be eliminated.
- If the number of software licenses can be reduced, on-going maintenance fees can be lower.

The potential for savings is specific to each enterprise and to each information technology operation. The point of the examples is to illustrate some obvious ways in which cost can be reduced.

Administrative cost savings potential

An inventory of storage and data is one of the starting points for assessing an enterprise's current state of storage management. The second, and potentially more significant starting point, is an inventory of storage management tasks and their cost, measured in administrative time and frequency of occurrence. Table 8-2 lists some common storage management tasks.

Table 8-2 Inventory of storage management tasks

Task	What's included
Storage configuration	Configuration of virtual storage devices as required by application and database servers

Table 8-2 Inventory of storage management tasks *(continued)*

Task	What's included
Storage network management	Zoning and LUN masking to make configured storage accessible by the hosts to which it is assigned; management of multiple access paths between hosts and storage devices
Data protection-related tasks	Creation, migration, and deletion of snapshots for backup, creation of replication groups, recovery testing
File management	Creation, expansion, migration, and deletion of file systems. Relocation of files to appropriate types of storage. Definition and monitoring of backup, replication, and relocation schedules

Tasks such as those listed in Table 8-2 should be inventoried with respect to the time they consume, their frequency of occurrence, and the level of administrative skill they require. Level of administrative skill provides a rough estimate of administrative cost per hour.

Multiplying these three factors together gives an estimate of total administrative cost for a given task. For example, if an enterprise creates weekly snapshots of databases on ten systems of three different platform types, using disk array techniques for two of them and a host-based technique for the third, the monthly cost for this task might be estimated approximately as illustrated in Table 8-3.

Table 8-3 Monthly cost of a single storage management task

Task	Occurrences per month	Cost per occurrence	Total cost
Timefinder snapshots	12 (3 systems x 4 weeks)	2 hours @ $95	$2,280
HDS snapshots	20 (5 systems x 4 weeks)	1.5 hours @ $75	$2,250
Host-based snapshots	8 (2 systems x 4 weeks)	1 hour @ $60	$480
		Grand total (per month)	$5,010

As the third column of Table 8-3 suggests, using different tools to perform a task or performing the task on different platforms might result in different administrative cost due to the level of skill required and the frequency with which the task is performed.

Cost estimates such as this hypothetical one can be prepared for all significant storage management tasks performed by data center administrators. The estimates provide the basis for calculating the savings potential of standardizing storage management tools, techniques, and processes.

Quality of service

Perhaps the most difficult to quantify of the three types of benefits of storage management standardization is the improvement in quality of service that can be delivered to the enterprise. Improved quality of storage service can stem from several sources. Table 8-4 suggests four common ways in which standardized storage management can improve the quality of the storage services an IT organization provides to its users.

Table 8-4 Reasons for improved quality of storage service

Quality of service metric	Reasons for improvement
I/O performance	Storing data on devices more appropriate to its value to the enterprise; Balancing I/O load more evenly across storage and network resources
Availability	Fewer application outages due to failed storage devices; Shorter application outages due to increased administrator familiarity with management tasks; Less downtime due to use of snapshots for on-host and off-host ancillary processing
Recovery from corruption	Shorter recovery point and recovery time objectives due to more frequent snapshots and fast resynchronization with corrupted data sets
Disaster recovery	Shorter recovery point and recovery time objectives due to replication of critical data to recovery location and automation of post-disaster application restart

Each of the quality of service metrics listed in Table 8-4 has a business value that can be quantified in terms of time—more transactions processed per day per employee due to better I/O performance, fewer lost sales or customers due to storage-related downtime; more goodwill retained or gained due to rapid recovery from disaster, and so forth. Each metric will be of different value to each enterprise. These and other similar potential quality of service improvements should be evaluated in terms of the positive value of storage management standardization.

The two faces of storage management standardization

Armed with knowledge of current capital costs, operating costs, and potential quality of service improvements, an IT organization can estimate the degree to which storage management standardization can be of benefit to it. Standardization of storage management takes two forms:

- Outward-facing standardization is the rationalization of the storage services delivered to client organizations
- Inward-facing standardization is the rationalization of the IT processes used to deliver storage services

Outward-facing standardization

Outward-facing standardization means delivering a standard menu of storage services to client organizations rather than specific devices configured in a client-specific way. For example, after surveying its client organizations' needs, an IT department might decide to provide four classes of service:

- non-redundant volumes
- RAID5-protected volumes
- Mirrored volumes
- Mirrored and replicated volumes

Based on analysis of storage consumption client it might decide to offer these four classes of storage in units of 100 gigabytes and 250 gigabytes.

Outward-facing standardization delivers capacity of a given quality to users rather than devices. It helps control cost by making existing storage components interchangeable with one another. In the short term, it increases the utility of whatever storage hardware exists in the data center by making virtual capacity based on it available to any user who requires it. In the longer term, standardizing storage service offerings introduces a level of discipline in clients that facilitates storage planning and service delivery. It enables an IT organization to be flexible in introducing new and different technologies to the data center because the services delivered to clients remain the same.

Inward-facing standardization

Inward-facing standardization is the rationalization of the components and tools used to implement the standard outward-facing offerings. It is here that immediate operating cost savings can be realized by reducing the number of tools and types of hardware used to deliver storage services, and in the longer term by aligning the installed storage hardware base more closely with enterprise data requirements.

Each storage management tool eliminated means immediate savings in license and maintenance cost. As administrators devote more of their time to working with a smaller set of tools, proficiency increases. The ultimate result is both increased efficiency and improved service quality due to fewer errors.

Implementing storage management standardization

Typically, IT organizations can implement outward-facing storage management standards faster than inward-facing ones, because the former are less capital-intensive. Moreover, by limiting the number and type of storage services offered, outward-facing standardization simplifies the requirements placed on the tools and hardware components that comprise the inward-facing phase. Ultimately, however, inward-facing standardization is where the operating cost savings come from. Thus, a move toward storage management standardization necessarily has two parts.

An IT organization that is convinced that it can deliver benefit to the enterprise by standardizing storage management should take certain steps to make sure that standardization is meaningful, and not an academic exercise.

Making outward-facing standards work

Like any form of utility computing, storage management standardization cannot be accomplished by the IT organization alone. Not only must an IT organization be convinced of the benefits, but its clients must become believers as well. The logical consequence is that all stakeholders in the enterprise must be part of the goal-setting, benefits analysis, and risk assessment that precede actual implementation of standards-based storage management. In this context, all stakeholders means not only IT clients, but also the executive and financial management of the enterprise, as well as the architecture, implementation, and operations components of the IT organization itself.

Part of the reason for broad enterprise involvement in the definition of outward-facing standards is to make sure that they meet clients' true storage needs. User departments that have a voice in defining standards are more likely to accept them when they are imposed, and more importantly, are more likely to find ways to use the standard services rather than demanding one-time special services that may have greater consequences for the enterprise than for the department that requests them.

Equally important in ensuring storage management standards are adhered to is the creation of barriers to non-conformance. An IT organization must steer a narrow course between being an effective service to the enterprise's business units and controlling the cost of information technology. On the one hand, it must meet the information technology requirements of the business, but on the other, it must enforce some level of discipline to avoid cost escalation due to unwarranted specialization.

Client organizations can be encouraged to follow storage standards in several ways. For example, standard operating procedure should be that requests for non-standard services be accompanied by written justification explaining why the standard services (which the client organization has helped to create) cannot serve the purpose. Such requests should be made visible at the executive level, perhaps to a data storage strategy oversight committee whose responsibility is to ensure on the one hand that standards are adhered to wherever possible, and on the other hand that standards remain relevant to the needs of the business.

The IT organization itself should have a standard means of estimating the lifetime cost of non-standard storage services. Lifetime cost estimates should include both hardware and software acquisition and on-going maintenance, but also the administrative cost of specialization—training, skill maintenance, and loss of administrative versatility. The full cost of non-standard services should be made visible at the executive and data storage oversight committee levels. Admittedly, some of these costs are speculative and difficult to quantify, but they are nevertheless an important part of the total cost of not adhering to standards.

Making inward-facing standards work

In some ways, the IT organization itself is the greatest challenge to standardization. Administrators inevitably develop attachment to the platforms and components for which they are responsible. They feel that their platform and tool-specific expertise is the value they have to offer the organization. For storage management standardization to succeed, administrative staff must feel empowered rather than threatened by it. For example, early in the inward-facing standardization process, training in the tools and platforms selected as standards should be readily available to administrators who specialize in components that will ultimately be phased out. Ideally, these administrators should be paired with "buddies" who can help them develop the new skills and experience by actual practice.

From here to standardization

Enterprise digital data storage is expensive and complex. It is unrealistic to expect an overnight transition from ad hoc storage management to a standards-based operation. An important component of success is the transition plan. Transition must balance timeliness, so that benefits can start being realized, against disruption, so that the enterprise can conduct business as usual during the transition.

Planning the transition to standard storage management

As described earlier, both outward-facing storage service offerings and inward-facing implementations must be well-thought out so that they meet current and anticipated enterprise needs. Storage offerings proposed as standards should be thoroughly tested, both with regard to functional correctness and suitability to purpose, and with respect to how quickly and smoothly they can be configured and placed into operation. Certain Storage Foundation advanced capabilities such as online migration of data between disk arrays and online expansion and shrinkage of file systems can play a large role in smoothing the transition to a standards-based storage management environment.

A detailed application-by-application plan for the transition to standards-based managed storage is a basic requirement of the transition. The plan should balance between risk and payback in several dimensions:

- Criticality of applications to the enterprise's conduct of business. For example, the impact of a 3-day outage of a retailer's point of sale system would obviously be intolerable, whereas a 3-day outage of its human resources system is probably survivable.
- Complexity of the transition. For example, a switch from disk array-based long-distance replication to VxVM-based replication is typically considerably more complex than a switch from disk array-based mirrored LUNs to VxVM-based virtual volumes whose mirrors are LUNs in two different arrays.
- Readiness of application and administrative staff. For example, experienced administrators may be designated to assist others as they go through their first transition to the new tools and offerings. As administrator and user experience grows, it becomes less risky to undertake more complex aspects of the transition.

There is no universally right answer to introducing new IT processes of any kind. Organizations that are primarily driven by cost reduction goals tend to be more aggressive, prioritizing applications for transition based on potential savings. More conservative organizations tend to prioritize applications for transition according to the potential impact of service disruption, at least until they have sufficient experience with the tools and techniques of standard storage to be comfortable with the transition process. Each enterprise must set priorities based on what is most important to it.

Hints for successful deployment

Whatever priorities an enterprise sets for transitioning to standards-based storage management, strong consideration should be given to a policy limiting new server deployments to standard storage tools and service offerings. New servers must be provisioned with storage somehow. Their users are less likely to have entrenched practices and expectations than users of existing systems.

Another prudent practice in implementing storage standardization is to implement in small steps. While improving quality of service by utilizing advanced features may be attractive, a more conservative approach which is more likely to succeed is to convert basic functions to the standards, and then add features incrementally as the experience base expands. For example, encapsulating existing LUNs as VxVM volumes and converting existing file systems to VxFS ones typically does not alter applications or operating procedures significantly. However, it lays the groundwork both for using basic Storage Foundation features, such as online data movement and coordinated volume and file system expansion, and for offering users more advanced capabilities, such as space-saving snapshots and dynamic multi-pathing.

Using Dynamic Storage Tiering for rapid payback

That having been said, one advanced Storage Foundation feature deserves particular consideration for early implementation–the Dynamic Storage Tiering (DST) facility. Dynamic Storage Tiering offers immediate reduction in the average cost of online storage, and is completely transparent to applications and storage utilities such as backup.

Following administrator-defined policies, Dynamic Storage Tiering automatically places new files on storage devices that are commensurate with the files' business value, and relocates files to different devices as their requirements or value change. Because DST does its work within the confines of a single file system name space, it is completely transparent to applications.

DST supports very general multi-tier storage hierarchies, but it delivers the most significant savings with a simple two-tier strategy. For most enterprises, the majority of online files are accessed infrequently. DST discovers and relocates inactive files to less-expensive second-tier storage. Because DST maps storage tiers to administrator-defined sets of VxVM volumes, administrators can define storage tiers and file placement policies once, and replace physical storage devices as business, economic and technology conditions make replacement appropriate with no policy alterations.

Using DST does not even require new hardware. For example, most disk array LUNs can be configured either as mirrored or RAID5. Administrators can define top-tier storage to be VxVM volumes based on mirrored LUNs, and second tier storage to be volumes based on RAID5 LUNs. DST can automatically move data to the RAID5 LUNs as it becomes inactive. With so-called "3+1" RAID5 LUNs consisting of four disk drives, the cost per byte of storing inactive data is immediately reduced by 33%. With larger RAID5 configurations, the savings are greater.

When the time comes to replace the devices upon which the original volumes are based, basic Storage Foundation facilities can be used to copy original LUN contents to replacement LUNs while the data is in use, even if the replacement LUNs are of different types than the ones they are replacing. Thus, introducing DST early leads to immediate payback in storage hardware savings, as well as setting the stage for delivering higher quality storage services with less disruption as requirements change and as old hardware is phased out in favor of new.

More storage standardization, more Storage Foundation value

As a data center's transition to standardized storage management practices gains momentum, Storage Foundation advanced features becomes more valuable. For example, with hundreds or thousands of LUNs to configure, virtualize, and allocate to servers, Intelligent Storage Provisioning can speed up storage deployment, reduce errors, and guarantee that an enterprise's intent for virtual storage is met. Similarly, Storage Foundation Management Server centralizes management of all Storage Foundation-related objects (disks, volumes, file systems, databases, servers, and applications), providing the data center-wide visibility that makes informed management decisions and actions possible. Even basic Storage Foundation features deliver increased value as deployment increases:

- Disk array-based synchronous replication over distances of a few kilometers can be supplanted by VxVM-based mirroring using long-distance Fibre Channel network links, eliminating on-going costs for replication software.
- Similarly, disk-array-based snapshot facilities can be replaced by Storage Foundation-based ones. Space-saving snapshots can reduce hardware cost of frequent snapshots, and make it possible to test recovery scenarios with minimal impact on operations. Storage Foundation snapshots can be placed on second-tier storage, reducing hardware cost further. Not only do Storage Foundation snapshots eliminate the on-going cost of disk array-based snapshot software, but data in Storage Foundation snapshots can be shared by platforms of different types because of the Portable Data Container facility.
- As single-purpose and single-platform tools are gradually eliminated, license, on-going maintenance, and training costs decrease.
- As single-purpose tools are eliminated, more administrative talent becomes focused on standard Storage Foundation-based procedures that are applicable

across all computing and storage platforms, increasing administrative versatility, and reducing the occurrence of errors that stem from unfamiliarity.

- Increased automation of simple administrative operations like volume creation and expansion, virtual storage reorganization, and so forth frees administrative talent for more strategic purposes such as performance analysis, capacity planning, and evaluation of new technologies.

For most purposes, Storage Foundation virtual volumes are equivalent to disk array-based LUNs. This facilitates the periods of parallel operation of old and new storage facilities that must necessarily precede transition to new components or operating procedures.

Summary: standardizing on the Storage Foundation

The value of standardizing the management of storage across the data center is undeniable. As the amount of data that enterprises keep online grows, management of it and the storage it occupies increases as a percentage of information technology budgets. One obvious way to attack the cost of storage management is to reduce its complexity, by reducing the number of different storage services offered and the number of tools and procedures required to implement them.

Earlier chapters discuss the value proposition of the Veritas Storage Foundation by Symantec:

- Complete basic and advanced storage management functionality in a single package
- Common storage management paradigm for major UNIX and Linux computing platforms as well as major disk arrays and storage network components
- Centralized management with a global view of data center storage that enables informed storage management decisions and actions
- Integration within the storage management software stack as well as with adjacent storage and data applications reduces the complexity of storage management tasks

Thus, the Veritas Storage Foundation is a primary candidate for bringing increasing storage management costs under control by simplifying, streamlining, and automating common storage management tasks, as well as by creating opportunities for IT organizations to deliver improved storage service quality to their business unit clients. As this chapter demonstrates, transition to Storage Foundation-based standardized storage management practices can be custom-designed to meet the needs and conform to the priorities of any enterprise IT organization. The Veritas Storage Foundation by Symantec deserves serious consideration by any enterprise that wishes to bring its information technology cost under control.